Garlinghouse Families

and Allied Families 1746–1996

Charles A. and Wilhelmine E. Garlinghouse

HERITAGE BOOKS
2013

HERITAGE BOOKS
AN IMPRINT OF HERITAGE BOOKS, INC.

Books, CDs, and more—Worldwide

For our listing of thousands of titles see our website
at
www.HeritageBooks.com

Published 2013 by
HERITAGE BOOKS, INC.
Publishing Division
5810 Ruatan Street
Berwyn Heights, Md. 20740

International Standard Book Numbers
Paperbound: 978-0-7884-1122-9
Clothbound: 978-0-7884-9053-8

Dedicated to Gail W. Rysso

Without her inspiration and help this book would not have been published.

TABLE OF CONTENTS

Foreward....................................vii

Garlinghouse Names, 1746-1996

A...................................1

B...................................11

C...................................17

D...................................26

E...................................33

F...................................46

G...................................51

H...................................58

I...................................63

J...................................67

K...................................83

L...................................86

M...................................98

N...................................111

O...................................115

P...................................118

R...................................121

S...................................129

T...................................138

U...................................141

V...................................142

W...................................145

Z...................................149

Index of Allied Names........................151

FOREWORD

"Garlinghouse is a long name and a strong name..." so starts the newspaper clipping from an unknown source dated 21 October 1849. The newspaper is probably from the town of Canandaigua, Ontario County in New York state.

Because so much of the history of this family has been unrecorded or lost, perhaps we should just leave that unidentified quote as a moot memorial to all those Garlinghouse ancestors who seem to have had an intense desire to live and die incognito. We think they would approve. There simply is no other explanation of the many Garlinghouses who were born, lived and died in this world, then virtually disappeared, leaving no wake, and very few records to mark their passing, or their very existence on the face of the earth.

This book lists more than a thousand of them who lived in America between 1746 and 1996. They are entered alphabetically by first name, whether they were born Garlinghouse or married a Garlinghouse. It also contains a surname index identifying more than a thousand members of allied families whose names appear in this book and their relationship to the Garlinghouse families into which they married.

The search to locate and identify them all has been a long and painstaking endeavor.

The earliest public record we found

referring to Garlinghouse is in the "Pennsylvania Archives." A copy of that record is also found on page 87 in "The History of Bucks County", by W. H. Davis (1905).

It states that on the 8th of June, 1746 the inhabitants living on the North Branch of the Delaware River, including Jonathon Garlinghous (sic), and the thirty-six families in Hunter's Settlement, petitioned the Court of Quarter Sessions of Bucks County, Pennsylvania. The petition "begged" the court, "...to lay off into a township, a district of country with the following boundaries: from the mouth of Tunam's creek up north branch of said creek upon the west side of Jeremiah Best's to the Blue Mountains: and thence by said mountains to ye north branch of said river: and thence by said branch to the mouth of said Tunam's creek again."

The same petition asked the court to lay out and open a road from Martin's mill to the Delaware.

The court ordered the petitioners to produce a draft of the township at the next term.

This movement led to the organization of Mt. Bethel Township within two years.

In 1746 another petition was sent to the Court of Quarter Sessions for the County of Bucks, requesting that a new township be established. It would be north of the "Zuydt" (Delaware River, to the Dutch). It would be called Smithfield Township. No action was taken on this petition, despite the fact that the settlements north of the mountains were accredited a population of five hundred "souls."

A second petition on behalf of Smithfield Township, in 1748, on which "John Garlinghouse" is one of the signatures, appears to have been successful. These two petitions are printed on pages 1048-1049 in "The History of Wayne, Pike & Monroe Counties, Pennsylvania."

On 18 February 1750 John George Gernhousen (sic) obtained a warrant to purchase fifty acres of land in Smithfield Township, Bucks County, Pennsylvania.

On page 85 of "Old Dansbury", by Ralf Ridgway Hillman, is a list of the inhabitants of Lower Smithfield Township, (1750-1755). Included in that list are J. G. Garlinghouse and James Garlinghouse. Hillman also suggests that J.G. is probably the father of James Garlinghouse.

As the size of the family increased, it expanded to the frontiers of the American continent. First to New Jersey, then to the Finger Lakes region of western New York: from there to Kentucky, Ohio, Michigan and Indiana. Then west to Illinois, Iowa and Missouri. One group homesteaded in Minnesota, another headed for Oregon. They were among the early wagon trains to cross the Rockies via the famed "Oregon Trail." A Garlinghouse family settled in Kansas, another in Colorado and New Mexico. We have found Garlinghouse families in California, Florida, Texas, Wisconsin and Hawaii. As they moved west they left descendants in all parts of the country.

Most of the early Garlinghouse families were farmers, which was customary, since they had to raise their own food. Others practiced trades that were essential for those early days: they were blacksmiths, wagonmakers, stone cutters and brick masons. Some were doctors or lawyers. Many became teachers.

Anna Parker, whose mother was Abigail Garlinghouse Parker, was the first school teacher in Avoca, New York in 1808.

Military service has been traditional in the Garlinghouse family. James Garlinghouse was wounded in a battle with Indians on 13 December 1755 during the French & Indian Wars.

Four Garlinghouse men served in the Revolutionary War, James and his three sons, John, Joseph and Benjamin. Benjamin also served during the Whiskey Rebellion in 1794.

Four sons of John Garlinghouse, Joseph, James L., John G. and Benjamin served in the War of 1812.

Many Garlinghouse men served during the Civil War. All were members of Union forces.

A large number served in the Spanish-American War, World Wars I and II: and many others fought in Korea, Viet Nam and Desert Storm.

Joseph Garlinghouse was appointed a U.S. Marshall to accompany the Cherokee Indians, for their protection, when they were forced to travel the "Trail of Tears" from the Carolinas to land west of the Mississippi River.

This is a brief sketch of the Garlinghouse family or families in America. The European "roots" have eluded us completely. We leave it to some future researcher to find them.

We ask you to help identify those Garlinghouses we missed. They should have been included here. We welcome any additions or corrections to our manuscript.

ABIGAIL - b. 1755, PA; d. 8 Apr 1813, Richmond Ctr., Ontario Co., New York; Buried in Richmond Ctr. Cem., Ontario Co., NY. Prob d/o James & Joanna (Buchanan) Garlinghouse. m. Nathaniel Parker about 1777, one child Anna. m2nd. John Johnson 1781, Sussex Co., NJ, children Jane, John, Andrew, Betsy, Johanna and Abigail.

ABIGAIL MARY - b. 8 Jul 1855, Allen's Hill, New York; d. 10 Nov 1950, Livonia, New York; Buried in St. Paul's Churchyard, Allen's Hill, Ontario Co., NY. d/o John Nelson & Lucy West (Bothwell) Garlinghouse. m. Charles Ward 30 Oct 1883, one child Irene.

ABRAHAM "ABRAM" - b. 15 Jan 1839, Grant Co., IN; d. 1913, Homer, Mich; Buried in Fairview Cemetery, Homer, MI. s/o Benjamin & Catherine Maria (Williams) Garlinghouse. m. Agnes A. (Rose) 3 Jul 1860, Topeka, Kan. children Raymond Edgar, Leona M. and Charles "Charly" Abram. m2nd. Mrs. Villa A. (Brooks) 29 Jun 1912, Battle Creek, Mich.

ACE - living at Surprise, AZ in 1996.

ACE NELSON - b. 25 Feb 1914, Halfway, Oregon; s/o Lyman Edwin & Ida Mae (Spaulding) Garlinghouse. m. Charlotte (Stone) 7 Aug 1936, children Carol Jean, Sandra Lee and Christie Lynn.

ACIL E. - b. 22 Jun 1856, Iowa; m. Julia C. (Stewart) 18 Jul 1908, Roseburg, Douglas Co., Oregon.

A. D. - b. 16 Aug 1905, Rockport, IN; d. 25 Apr 1928, Cherokee Co., TX; s/o Franklin Bennett

& Lilly M. (Grady) Garlinghouse.

ADA (...) - b. IL; m. Norman Fayette "Frank" Garlinghouse 16 Aug 1870, children Morris and Cyril. m2nd H.M. Hartzell.

ADA E. (Schmidt) - b. 18 Feb 1895; d. 7 Jan 1973, Spokane Wash; m. Samuel Dayton Garlinghouse Sep 1913, children Zona Pauline and Elaine Lurcil

ADELAIDE "ADDIE" - b. 1866, Allens Hill, Richmnd Twp., Ontario Co., New York; d. Dec 1930, Ontario Co., New York; d/o John Nelson & Lucy West (Bothwell) Garlinghouse. m. Elnathan "Nathaniel" Briggs, children Rodney N., Donald G. and Whitney.

ADELBERT E. - b. Aug 1859, Mich; d. 1938, Hillsdale, Co., Mich; s/o Ira Reed & Melissa A. (Coryell) Garlinghouse. m. Margaret L. (Eighney) Black 6 Apr 1892. m2nd. Affena (...) 1898, Mich.

ADELINE (King) - b. 1865, Canada; d. 1939, Chippewa Co., Mich; m. Ulysses Grant Garlinghouse 24 Mar 1891, Kinross, Chippewa Co., Mich.

AFFENA (...) - b. Apr 1882, Mich; m. Adelbert E. Garlinghouse 1898.

AGNES A. (Rose) - b. Dec 1842, Allen, Mich; d. 21 Jul 1911, Homer, Mich; Buried in Fairview Cemetery, Homer, Mich. m. Abraham "Abram" Garlinghouse 3 July 1860, Topeka, Kan, children Raymond Edgar, Leona M. and Charles "Charly" Abram.

AGNES (Oakland) - b. 30 Nov 1919, Bisbee, Towner Co., ND; m. Robert Erwin Garlinghouse 6 Dec 1941, St. Paul, Ramsey Co., Minn, children Roberta Agnes, Nancy Jeanne, Thomas Lee and Colleen Joanne.

ALBERT A. -m. P.(...). Living at Dickinson, TX in 1996.

ALBERT EDWARD - b. 22 Nov 1910; d. 12 Oct 1968; s/o Edward Sylvester & Emma (Shae) Garlinghouse. m. Lorraine (Fredericks), children Frederick and Carol.

ALBERT FREDERICK - b. 21 May 1892, Leadville, Colo; d. Sep 1973, South Pasadena, CA; s/o Holmes Spalding & Emma Permelia (Sherman) Garlinghouse. m. Ferne Beatrice (Armstrong) Aug 1915, Canon City, Colo, children Margaret "Peggy" Lee and Albert Frederick. m2nd. Marguerite (McNair) Devers 1951, Eagle Rock, CA.

ALBERT FREDERICK - b. 1933, Los Angeles, CA; s/o Albert Frederick & Ferne Beatrice (Armstrong) Garlinghouse. m. Barbara Evlyn (Myers) 1961, Los Angeles CA, children Frederick "Ricky" Myers, James Armstrong and Thomas Sherman.

ALBERT V. - s/o ... Garlinghouse. He was listed in Spokane, WA city directory in 1928.

ALICE - d/o Levi Curtis & Eva (Stuart) Garlinghouse. m. Floyd Armstrong.

ALICE - b. 1891, Kinross, Chippewa Co., Mich; d. 1975, W. VA; d/o Ulysses Grant Garlinghouse. m. Libourne W. Williams, children two daughters.

ALICE "ALLIE" - b. 1863, IN; d/o Cyrenus A. & Sarah A. (Jackson) Garlinghouse. m. Wm. H. Orahood, children Lillian G. and Grace.

ALICE BRUNDAGE - b. 30 Dec 1868, Wayne, Steuben Co., New York; d. 21 Mar 1897; d/o Daniel Benjamin & Sarah "Sally" (Margeson) Garlinghouse. m. C.A. Satterthwaite 10 Dec 1891.

ALICE C. (Vining) - b. 13 Jan 1852, Mich; d. 4 Oct 1937, Mich; m. ... Seaman. m2nd. John Coryell Garlinghouse 23 Dec 1896, Columbia, Jackson Co., Mich.

ALLISON KABLER - b. 12 Jan 1990; d/o Robert Bruce & Diana (Morgan) Garlinghouse.

ALMA JUNE (Weber) - m. Tilden Willard Garlinghouse.

ALMINA TILLIE - b. 16 Feb 1873, Shawnee Co., Kan; d/o Lucian Bonaparte & Matilda Ruth (Hanawalt) Garlinghouse. m. L. Bittle Bushong, M.D. 18 May 1898, one child Mina Ruth.

ALMOND JEWETT - b. 20 Nov 1869, Worthington, Iowa; d. 28 Apr 1951, Oregon; s/o Darius Hill & Minerva Jane "Jennie" (White) Garlinghouse. m. Laura Elma (Hayden) 29 Jun 1892, one child Harold Charles. m2nd. Margaret (Bloom) 1923.

ALOIS BRUCE - b. 15 Dec 1881, TX; d. Aug 1969, Vernon, TX; s/o Cyrus Buell & Amelia Florence (Fitzpatrick) Garlinghouse.

ALTA MARIA - b. 28 Nov 1848, Delaware, Ohio; d. 23 Sep 1929, Winfield, Kan; Buried at Dexter Cem., Cowley Co., Kan. d/o Silas & Margaret (Reid) Garlinghouse. m. John D. Maurer 22 Nov 1868, Lyon Co., Kan, children Ralph J., Willis R., Maud and Rowland Blaine.

ALVIN NATHAN - b. 2 May 1902, IN; s/o Edmond Oscar & Sarah (Wilson) Garlinghouse.

AMANDA (Belknap) - b. 1807, New York; d. 30 Mar 1882, Princeton, Mille Lacs Co., Minn; m. Josiah Garlinghouse 1827, KY, children Catherine, Lacy, Susannah "Rosanna", James Mitchell, Mary, Rachel and Henry

AMANDA - b. Dec 1894, Kinross, Chippewa Co., Mich; d/o Ulysses Grant Garlinghouse. m. H.

Wesley Bradey

AMANDA ROSE - b. 2 May 1976; d/o Kent Nelson & Rosemary (Gutierrez) Garlinghouse.

AMBER JOY - b. 1960; d/o Junior Ellsworth & Lucy (Gascho) Garlinghouse.

AMELIA (Webb) - b. 10 Apr 1815, Vernon, Sussex Co., NJ; d. 8 Jul 1872, N. Milford, Orange Co., NY; m. George Garlinghouse, children Martha, Mary, Anna "Ann" and Amelia Orvilla.

AMELIA FLORENCE (Fitzpatrick) - b. 7 Jun 1857, Memphis, Tenn; d. 10 Mar 1941, Crowell, TX; m. Cyrus Buell Garlinghouse, Jr. 31 Jul 1879, Sherman, TX, children Lele Efagenia, Alois Bruce and Elmer Buell.

AMELIA M. (...) - b. 1853-54; d. 20 Feb 1894, Chicago, Cook Co., IL; Buried in Milwaukee, Wisc. m. Charles A. Garlinghouse.

AMELIA "AURILLA" ORVILLA - b. 1849; d. 1937; d/o George & Amelia (Webb) Garlinghouse. m. Nathaniel Weller 5 Oct 1874, Old Dutch Church, Kingston, New York, children Flora M. and Frances.

AMELIA S. - b. 12 Jan 1834, Richmond, New York; d. 9 Jul 1845, Richmond, New York; d/o Joseph & Submit (Sheldon) Garlinghouse.

AMELIA S. - b. 1845, Canandaigua, Ontario Co., New York; d. 16 Jan 1847, Canandaigua, Ontario Co., New York; d/o Leman B. & Martha Ann (Spalding) Garlinghouse.

AMERICA J. (Bradburn) - b. 1852, KY; m. Andrew Leonard Garlinghouse 31 Dec 1865, Denver, Colo, children Henry, George B., Lucy and Elias Buell.

AMY - b. 16 Sep 1820, Sussex Co., NJ; d/o Thomas & Polly "Mary" (Benjamin)

Garlinghouse.

ANADELLA - d/o George Arza Garlinghouse.

ANDREW LEONARD - b. Jun 1833, OH; d. 10 Mar 1905, Montezuma, Colorado; He served in the Civil War from 1 Dec 1861 to 5 Sep 1862 as Corporal in Company I of the 54th Illinois Volunteers. s/o John G. & Lewanna (Bennett) Garlinghouse. m. Sarah Ann (Ratcliff) 31 Jul 1856, Van Buren Co., Iowa, children Elias M., George M., Lenora Regina plus one male. m2nd. America J. (Bradburn) 31 Dec 1865, Denver, CO, children Henry, George B., Lucy and Elias Buell.

ANN - b. May 1957, Geneva, IL; d/o Ralph Spalding & Ellen (Ekman) Garlinghouse.

ANN - living at Long Lake, Minn in 1996.

ANN ELIZA(BETH) - b. 2 Sep 1833, Licking Co., Ohio; d. 9 Mar 1912, Terre Haute, Vigo Co., IN; d/o James L. & Susannah (Belknap) Garlinghouse. m. James Steed 27 Mar 1855, at home of Addison Carter in Licking Co., Ohio, children Melissa E. and Della. m2nd. Elias Horner 3 May 1896, W. Union, IL.

ANNA "ANN" - b. 1847; d/o George & Amelia (Webb) Garlinghouse.

ANNA (Bennet) - m. James Garlinghouse, children Willard, Ira David, Mary "May" and Eva.

ANNA (...) - b. 16 May 1885; d. Apr 1974, McMinnville, TN; m. ... Garlinghouse.

ANNA - b. about 1907; d/o Franklin Bennett & Lilly M. (Grady) Garlinghouse.

ANNA (...) - m. Dale Garlinghouse. Living at Jacksonville, FL in 1996.

ANNA B. (Jones) - b. 7 Oct 1881, TX; d. Dec

1975, Lewiston, Idaho; m. Arthur Richard Garlinghouse 30 Oct 1901, Sedan, Kan, children George Arza, Nita Cora and Richard Lynn.

ANNA E. "Anna May" - b. 21 Oct 1872, Jackson, Mich; d. 12 Feb 1921, Napoleon, Mich; d/o Ira Reed & Melissa A (Coryell) Garlinghouse. m. Frank J. Louden 1 Jan 1890, Napoleon, Mich, children Forest, Anah, Ila, George and Frances Cordelia.

ANNA LOUISE - b. May 1870, Mt. Morris, Livingston Co., New York; d. 18 Sep 1901, Clinton, New York; Buried in Sunset Hill Cem., Clinton, NY. d/o Joseph & Chloe Rebecca (Beardsley) Garlinghouse. m. Edward Byron Stanley 26 Jun 1894, Clinton, New York.

ANNA M. (Robertson) - m. John Garlinghouse.

ANNE (Morehouse) - b. 1762; d. 1840-1850, Penn Yan, Yates Co., New York; m. Benjamin Garlinghouse Mar 1781, children Stephen A., Samuel S., Sarah Elizabeth, Julia Ann and Peter.

ANNE (Stark) - m. Martin Leroy Garlinghouse.

ANNE PATRICIA - b. 5 Aug 1943; d/o Wendell & Ella Helen (Skadeen) Garlinghouse. m. ... Reamon, children Todd and Derek.

ANTHONY - m. Lenore (...) living at Monticello, Minn in 1996.

ARABELLA (BELLE) LOUISE - b. 4 Mar 1842, Allen's Hill, Richmond Twp., Ontario Co., New York; d. 10 Jul 1897, Chicago, IL; Buried in Belvidere Cem., Belvidere, IL. d/o John Nelson & Lorinda (Short) Garlinghouse. m. Lt. Col. Lemuel O. Gilman 4 Dec 1884, Chicago, IL.

ARDYCE LORAINE - b. 5 Jul 1935; d/o Carroll &

Velma Mae (Shirkey) Garlinghouse. m. Herman G. Obst 28 Aug 1956, one child David Wayne.

ARLENE RUTH - b. 18 Dec 1894, Madison, Jefferson Co., TN; d/o Ulysses Arthur & Mary Erskine (Davis) Garlinghouse. m. Frederick Henry Linnemeier 3 Oct 1936

ARNET JOHN - b. 25 Mar 1888, Raisin Twp., Lenawee Co., Mich; d. Jun 1974, Miami, Dade Co., FL; s/o Gurdon Benedict & Minnie Minerva (Gates) Garlinghouse. m. Leona Mae (Beebe) 22 Oct 1910, Tipton, Mich, children Arnet John and Bruce Beebe. m2nd. Maude (Williams) 8 May 1941.

ARNET JOHN - b. 23 Oct 1920; s/o Arnet John & Leona Mae (Beebe) Garlinghouse. m. Jean (Stewart) 1944, children Susan, Janet and Kathleen. m2nd. Carol (Chaffin) 1965, one child Arnet John, III.

ARNET JOHN III - 16 Feb 1970; s/o Arnet John & Carol (Chaffin) Garlinghouse.

ARTHELIA JANE "Jennie" - b. 9 May 1842, Ohio; d. 25 Dec 1926, Topeka, Kan; d/o Silas & Margaret (Reid) Garlinghouse. m. George Sayler 1 Nov 1869, near Emporia, Kan.

ARTHUR s/o James L. & Susannah (Belknap) Garlinghouse.

ARTHUR ALDER - b. 27 Oct 1890, San Antonio, TX; d. 3 Jun 1974, Orlando, Orange Co., FL; Buried in Greenwood Cem., Orlando, FL. s/o Walter Sheldon & Julia Annie (Alder) Fisk Garlinghouse. m. Muriel Beatrice (Montgomery) 2 Nov 1914, Ponce, Puerto Rico, one child Arthur A., Jr. m2nd. Dora (Reyna) Castillo, Orlando, FL, one child Walter Sheldon, III.

ARTHUR ALDER, Jr. - b. 25 Dec 1915, St. Louis, MO; He served in World War II; s/o Arthur Alder & Muriel Beatrice (Montgomery)

Garlinghouse. m. Esther Jonsson, Fayetteville, Ark.

ARTHUR B. - b. Sep 1852, WI; s/o Benjamin & Catherine Maria (Williams) Garlinghouse. m. Ida "James J." (...), one son J. Merle.

ARTHUR L. - b. 9 Sep 1847, Canandaigua, New York; d. 19 Feb 1913, Arcade, New York; s/o Leman B. & Martha Ann (Spalding) Garlinghouse. m. Carrie A. (Phillips) 1871, one child Frederick L. m2nd. Sarah M. (Baker), children Olive D., Leon "Leman" B., Layman, a daughter and Fred Lee.

ARTHUR RICHARD - b. 4 Nov 1877, Independence, Kan; d. 3 Apr 1959, Lewiston, Idaho; s/o Arza H. & Sarah "Sadie" Elaine (Holmes) Garlinghouse. m. Anna B. (Jones) 30 Oct 1901, Sedan, Kan, children George Arza, Nita Cora and Richard Lynn.

ARVILLA (Lawrence) - b. 30 Jan 1858, NY; d. 9 Oct 1921, Calhoun Co., Mich; m. ... Brooks. One child Allio L. m2nd. Abraham "Abram" Garlinghouse 29 Jun 1912, Battle Creek, Mich.

ARZA H. - b. 29 Jun 1850, IL; d. 11 Dec 1922, Lewiston, Idaho; s/o Benjamin & Catherine Maria (Williams) Garlinghouse. m. Sarah "Sadie" Elaine (Holmes) Mar 1873, children Arthur Richard, Gerald Arza, Hazel "Hec" "Hasel" Rupert and Georgia.

AUDREY G. - b. 1906, Clarkston, Wash; d/o Gerald Arza & Elizabeth (Gilbert) Garlinghouse. m. ... Pease, one child David.

AUGUSTA (Demmett) - b. about 1822, VA; m. Thomas Briggs Garlinghouse 1847, children Louise and Harriet.

AURELIUS DEWITT - b. 24 Feb 1844, IN; d. 8 Aug 1913, Rockport, Spencer Co., IN; He served in the Civil War from 2 Aug 1863 to 24 Feb 1864 as Sergeant in Company I, 117th Regiment of Indiana Volunteer Infantry. s/o George Bennett & Isabella Jolly (DeWitt) Garlinghouse. m. Mary (de Bruler) 13 Dec 1869, children Lucy Livings and Franklin Bennett.

AXIE "ACHSA" MABLE (Yingling) - b. 2 Dec 1868, PA, but "of TX"; d. 12 Apr 1962, Hidalgo Co., TX; m. Elbannis Carroll Garlinghouse 11 Nov 1891, children Mildred and Carroll.

BARBARA - (...) -m. Dale Lee Garlinghouse. Living at Marion, Iowa in 1966.

BARBARA EVLYN (Myers) - m. Albert Frederick Garlinghouse 1961, Los Angeles, CA, children Frederick "Ricky" Myers, James Armstrong and Thomas Sherman.

BARBARA IRENE (Frame) m. Grant Wesley Garlinghouse 1956, Newton, Iowa, children Wanda Leilana and Keith David.

BARBARA J. - b. 19 Apr 1972, Bell Co., TX; d/o ... Garlinghouse.

BARBARA JEAN - b. 7 Apr 1962, Sault Ste. Marie, Mich; d/o Frederick Mark & Doris Margaret (Long) Garlinghouse.

BARBARA L. (Owens) - b., Alabama; m. Lyle David Garlinghouse, one child Tracy Lynn.

BARBARA LEIGH - b. 1935; d/o Elton Elsworth & Leona (Beckman) Garlinghouse. m. Joseph Anthony Bekes 1954, children Stephanie Ann, Michael Joseph and Gerald Allen.

BARN - living at Topeka, KS in 1996

BELLE (McBride) - m. Samuel Dayton Garlinghouse 1 May 1902, children Elmer George and Fern L.

BENJAMIN - b. 1761, Hardyston, Sussex Co., NJ; d. 6 Feb 1850, Penn Yan, Yates Co., New York; His tombstone is located in Hunt's Hollow Cemetery, south-west of Naples, Ontario Co.,NY. He served in the Revolutionary War from 15 June 1778 to 4 Mar 1783 as Private in

Captain Helm's Company, 2nd New Jersey Regiment, commanded by Colonel Israel Shreve. Also in Captain John N. Cumming's Company and Captain Samuel Reading's Company commanded by Colonel Elias Dayton. Also 1st Company, 2nd New Jersey Regiment commanded by Colonel Elias Dayton, Lt. Colonel Francis Barber and Lt. Colonel John N. Cumming. He also served during the Sullivan Expedition against the Iroquois Nation, in 1779, as Private in Captain Samuel Reading's Company. During the Pennsylvania Insurrection (The Whiskey Rebellion), he served from 11 Sep 1794 to 24 Dec 1794 as Private in Captain John C. Crane's Company, 2nd Regiment of Infantry. He is probably s/o James & Joanna (Buchanan) Garlinghouse. m. Anne (Morehouse) Mar 1781, children Stephen A., Samuel S., Sarah Elizabeth, Julia Ann and Peter.

BENJAMIN- b. 1791; d. 28 Dec 1812, Ontario Co., New York; Buried in St. Paul's Churchyard, Allen's Hill, Ontario Co., New York. He served in the War of 1812 from 27 Sep 1812 to 10 Nov 1812 in Captain Elizur Hill's Company of Light Infantry. He died as a result of a service connected illness. s/o John & Jane (Leonard) Garlinghouse.

BENJAMIN - b. 1810-15, Ontario Co., New York; s/o James L. & Susannah (Belknap) Garlinghouse.

BENJAMIN - b. 1815, near Onandaga, New York; d. Kansas; s/o John G. & Lewanna (Bennett) Garlinghouse. He was a stone cutter. m. Catherine Maria (Williams) 11 Jan 1837, Ohio, children Dau., Abraham A. "Abram", George C., Parker., Arza H., Arthur B. and Jeremiah "Gerald".

BENJAMIN PORTER - b. 24 Sep 1911, Lebanon, Montezuma Co., Colo; d. 23 Apr 1963, Dallas, TX; s/o Elias Buell & Virda Ellen (Lucas) Garlinghouse. m. Mrs. Imogene (Shaw) Ferguson

1938.

BENSON J - b. 11 Jul 1860, Lenawee Co., Mich; d. 24 May 1908, Mich; He was twin to Burton A. s/o John Benedict & Mary Jane (Benedict) Garlinghouse. m. Margaret C. (Gray) 26 Nov 1895, Mich, children Burton A. and John G.

BERTHA E. (...) - b. 29 Mar 1917; d. Jan 1984, Centralia, Wash; m. ... Price. m2nd. James Rufus Garlinghouse 7 Feb 1970, Tacoma, Wash.

BERTHA MAY - b. 19 Nov 1871, Emporia, Lyon Co., Kan; d/o Lewis N. & Nancy Jane "Jennie" (Lockerman) Garlinghouse. m. Henry Thomas Read @ 1893, children Harold T. and two, who died young.

BERTHA T. (Gerrels) - b. 15 Jan 1893; d. 30 Oct 1979, Southfield, Mich; She was killed in an auto accident. m. Bryan Hess Garlinghouse 8 Oct 1921, children Shirley Ann and Viola.

BESS - b. 1880, IN; d/o John Francis Oscar & Mary E. (McClure) Garlinghouse. m. Hugh Heberhart.

BESSIE (...) m. Jeremiah "Gerald" Garlinghouse B/4 1900, children Lynn and Treva.

BESSIE - b. 4 Feb 1915, Aitkin Co., Minn; d/o William Josiah & Elizabeth Howe (Campbell) Garlinghouse. m. David Millern.

BETH - d/o Robert Lee & Jean (...) Garlinghouse.

BETTY (Finley) - m. Wallace Elias "Wally" Garlinghouse, one child Ronnie.

BETTY JO - b. 21 Aug 1926, Madison, IN; d/o George Howard & Mildred (Jones) Garlinghouse. m. Stanley Kroll 24 Dec 1942, children Gloris Jean, Stanley Andrew, Vicky Lee and Beverley Ann.

BETTY LOIS (Bone) - b. 8 Sep 1913, Ohio; d. 16 Nov 1987, San Francisco, CA; m. Leland Eugene Garlinghouse.

BETSY JEAN (Anderson) - b. 1926; m. Edwin Oscar Garlinghouse 26 Apr 1946, children Peter Lynn, Dale Lee and Paul Ray.

BETSY LYNN - b. 1975; d/o Peter Lynn & Pamela Jean (Hollingsworth) Garlinghouse.

BEVERLY (Worlock) - m. Harold James Garlinghouse, Jr.

BEVERLY ANN - b. 1934; d/o Ira Birchfield & Iva Mable (Abeare) Garlinghouse. m. Larry Earl Scheddel 1954, children Gary Lee, Joel Larry, Lori Ann, Jack Lester, Jery Loren and Greg Larry.

B. G. - Living in San Diego, CA in 1996.

B. K. - living at Topeka, KS in 1996.

B. K. - Living at Vail, CO in1996.

BILL - s/o ... Garlinghouse. m. Nerine (...). Living at Olathe, CO in 1996.

BONNIE (Crumback) - b. 1936; m. Eugene Wayne Garlinghouse 1953, children Sherie, Randy, Chris and Larry.

BRADLEY GENE - s/o Mark & Elizabeth Victoria (Pope) Garlinghouse.

BRADLEY KENT - b. 1 Aug 1941; s/o Francis Mark & Marjorie Cosper (Beard) Garlinghouse. m. Susan Buder (Horan) 29 Jun 1963, St. Louis, Mo.,@ 1965, children Kimberly Anne, Marjorie Elise, Joseph Mark, Bradley Kent, Jr. and Matthew David.

BRADLEY KENT, JR. - b. 6 Feb 1971; s/o Bradley

Kent & Susan Buder (Horan) Garlinghouse.

BRENDA (...). m. Nathan Andrew Garlinghouse. Living at Madison, IN in 1996.

BRENDA JEAN - b. 1961; d/o Ralph Basil & Consuelo Hilda (Ramerz) Garlinghouse.

BRIAN - s/o Peter Lynn & Pamela Jean (Hollingsworth) Garlinghouse.

BRODERICK - living at Colonia, NJ in 1996.

BRUCE - living at Malta, MT in 1996.

BRUCE - m. Patricia (...). living at Boulder,CO in 1996.

BRUCE - b. Jul 1954, Geneva, IL; s/o Ralph Spalding & Ellen (Ekman) Garlinghouse.

BRUCE BEEBE - b. 26 Oct 1924, Lansing, Ingham Co., Mich; He served in World War II as Captain in US Navy. s/o Arnet John & Leona Mae (Beebe) Garlinghouse. m. Vivian Dickinson (Kabler) 22 Mar 1952, San Francisco, CA, children William J., Robert Bruce, Julie Ann and Carrie Lee.

BRUCE EDMUND - b. 1 Oct 1908, Coeur d'Alene, Idaho; s/o Edmund Oscar & Elizabeth Jane Allen (Bruce) Garlinghouse. m., one child Kent Armin.

BRYAN HESS - b. 27 Feb 1898, Homer, Mich; d. Mar 1984, Southfield, Mich; s/o Charly "Charles" Abram & Louise (Hess) Garlinghouse. m. Bertha T. (Gerrels) 8 Oct 1921, children Shirley Ann and Viola.

BUD - b. 1 Jun 1919, Aitkin Co., Minn; d. 8 May 1988, Centralia, Wash; s/o William Josiah & Elizabeth Howe (Campbell) Garlinghouse. m. Eloise (...).

BURTON A. - b. 11 Jul 1860, Lenawee Co., Mich; d. 1943, CA; twin to Benson J. s/o John Benedict & Mary Jane (Benedict) Garlinghouse. m. Irma (...). m2nd. Corrine (Sheldon) 1941. m3rd. Mrs. Gertrude (...) Richardi 25 Jul 1941, CA.

BURTON A. - b. 7 Apr 1898, Mich; d. May 1988, Pasadena, CA; d. 2 May 1988. s/o Benson J. & Margaret C. (Gray) Garlinghouse

CALISTA "Calissia" EMILY - b. 24 Jan 18

36, Ohio; d. 5 Feb 1919, Emporia, Kan; d/o Silas & Margaret (Reid) Garlinghouse. m. Matthew W. Kirkendall 24 Dec 1861, Van Buren Co., Iowa, children Omer A., George, and Cora.

CAROL - d/o Albert Edward & Lorraine (Fredericks) Garlinghouse. m. Robert Carter, 2 children.

CAROL - b. 1939; d/o John Raymond & Genevieve May (Aldread) Garlinghouse. m. Jerry Yager, children Jeffrey A., Scott T. and Kelly Lynn.

CAROL (Chaffin) - m. Arnet John Garlnghouse 1965, one child Arnet John, 3d.

CAROL - b. Ohio; d/o Mervyn W. "Bud" & Grace (...) Garlinghouse. m. Ronald Sabins. m2nd. ... Canode.

CAROL JEAN - b. 31 Aug 1940; d/o Ace Nelson & Charlotte (Stone) Garlinghouse. m. Walter Ball 24 Aug 1963, children Kathleen, Kristin and Kelly. m2nd. Ronald Everett.

CAROLINE - b. 1856, Canandaigua, Ontario Co., New York; d. 5 Sep 1894, Hornellsville, Steuben Co., NY; Buried in Lohin-Hamburg Cem., Hamburg, Erie Co., NY. d/o Leman B. & Martha Ann (Spalding) Garlinghouse. m. Alfred Augustus Houghton 7 May 1877, Buffalo, Erie Co., NY, children Katherine Martha, Edith and Marion.

CAROLINE "Callie" S. (Knorr) - b. Apr 1858, Ohio; d. 1920, Johnstown, Delaware Co., Ohio;

m. George E, Garlinghouse 3 Jul 1877, Delaware Co., Ohio, children Florence "Florina" A., Glenwood K. and Ethel Rose.

CAROLINE MARY - b. 1 Dec 1851, Sussex Co., NJ; d. 20 Feb 1902, Sussex Co., NJ; d/o John & Catherine Elizabeth (Utter) Garlinghouse. m. John Henry Williams 11 Nov 1874, children William E., Ethel, James H., Robert Albert, John M. and Kittie Elizabeth.

CAROLYN RUTH - d/o James Buell "Bub" & Ruth (Huckabay) Garlinghouse. m. Ronnie Stephens

CARON - d/o ... Garlinghouse. Living at Lebanon, OR in 1996.

CARRIE/ CARRY (...) - b. 1873-5, Germany; m. twice. m2nd John Edward Garlinghouse B/4 1920. She had one child Florence by first husband.

CARRIE (Wolcott) - b. Apr 1841, d. 1914, Mich; m. Daniel Benjamin Garlinghouse B/4 1873, children Lulu E. and Edna M.

CARRIE A. (Philips) - b. 12 Aug 1850, Bristol, New York; d. 29 Mar 1923, Perrinton, Monroe Co., New York; m. Arthur L. Garlinghouse 1871, one child Frederick L.

CARRIE MAE (Kingsbury) - b. 12 Sep 1888; d 23 Oct 1915; m. George Lovette Garlinghouse, one child George L., Jr.

CARRIE LEE - b. 8 Jun 1962; d/o Bruce Beebe & Vivian Dickinson (Kabler) Garlinghouse. m. Thomas C. Andrews 4 May 1985.

CARROLL - b. 22 Feb 1899; d. 23 Dec 1973, Donna, Hidalgo Co., TX; s/o Elbannis Carroll & Axie "Achsa" Mable (Yingling) Garlinghouse. m. Velma Mae (Shirkey), children Shirley Mae, Carroll Ellsworth, Earl Alonzo and Ardyce Loraine.

CARROLL ELLSWORTH - b. 17 Apr 1932; s/o Carroll and Velma Mae (Shirkey) Garlinghouse.

CARY - (...) - m. Charles Garlinghouse. Living at Pompano Beach, FL in 1996.

CASSIAH "KEZIAH" (Nichols) - b. 1814, Ohio; m. Cyrus Buell Garlinghouse 21 Oct 1832, Clinton Co., IN, children Cyrenus A., John G., Martin V., Cyrus Buell, Jr., Lewanna "Lovina", Evaline J. and Mariah "Maria" M.

CATHERINE - b. 16 Dec 1784, Luzerne Co., PA; d. 24 Jan 1872, Kilmore, Clinton Co., IN; d/o James & Elanor "Eleanor" (Hunt) Garlinghouse. m. Elijah Belknap 8 Jan 1806, Ontario Co., NY, children Amanda, James Mitchell, Samuel, Amazilla, Gamaliel, Esther, Jonas, Joseph Gillett, Mary Jane, Lafayette and Jane.

CATHERINE - b. 1828, Hart Co., KY; d. 6 Jan 1887, Aitkin, Minn; d/o Josiah & Amanda (Belknap) Garlinghouse. m. David Woodruff Garlinghouse 5 Jul 1849, Wapello Co., Iowa, children Jasper Sylvester, Lucretia D., David, Jr., Olive, Ulysses Grant, William Josiah, Sherman and Evalyn "Eva" "Evalina." m2nd. Asa Walbridge 2 Aug 1883, Sauk Rapids, Benton Co., Minn.

CATHERINE - b. 10 Jul 1829, NJ; d/o Joseph & Maria "Mary" (Ryerson) Garlinghouse. m. John W. Terhune 1849, Jersey City, NJ, children Ransfred "Ransford I" and Josephine.

CATHERINE ELIZABETH (UTTER) - b. 18 Mar 1825; d. 18 June 1879, Sussex Co., NJ; Buried at Warwick, NY; m. John Garlinghouse 2 Jan 1843 children Silas, John Monroe, Colina, Caroline Mary, Cathren J. and a female b. 10 July 1863.

CATHERINE M. (Spence) - b. 1917, Bayonne, NJ; d. 13 Oct 1958, Ellenville, New York; m.

Harold James Garlinghouse, children Patricia E., Harold James, Jr. and Edward Joseph.

CATHERINE MARIA (Williams) - b. 1815, Ohio; d. Litchfield, Mich, m. Benjamin Garlinghouse 11 Jan 1837, Franklin Co., Ohio, children dau., died at birth, Abraham "Abram", George C., Parker, Arza H., Arthur B. and Jeremiah "Gerald."

CATHREN J. - b. 15 Feb 1857, Vernon, Sussex Co., NJ; d/o John & Catherine Elizabeth (Utter) Garlinghouse

CATHY (...) m. William "Bill" Garlinghouse. Living at Sonoma, CA in 1996.

CECIL R. - b. Jan 1885, CA; d. 17 Sep 1937, Los Angeles Co., CA; s/o Stephen & Prudence W. (Howard) Garlinghouse.

CHARLENE - d/o Charles R. Garlinghouse.

CHARLES - m. Cary (...).living at Pompano Beach, FL in 1996.

CHARLES - b. 20 Sep 1864, NY; d. 24 Jun 1907, Hamptonburg, NY; s/o Thomas D. & Susan (Osborne) Garlinghouse.

CHARLES A. - b. Jan 1843, Canandaigua, Ontario Co., New York; d. 16 Jan 1890, LaCrosse, WI; He served in the Civil War from 28 July 1862 to 3 June 1865 as Lieutenant in Companies B and D, 126th Regiment, New York Infantry Volunteers. He was captured at Harper's Ferry 15 Sep 1862 and paroled the same date, also at Harper's Ferry. s/o Leman Benton & Martha Ann (Spalding) Garlinghouse. m. Mary Elizabeth (Hewitt), one child- Nettie. m2nd. Amelia M. (...).

CHARLES A.- b. 1862, Switzerland Co., IN; s/o John G. & Susan (Moody) Garlinghouse. m. Ellen (Courter) Downey 19 Nov 1884,

Switzerland Co., IN.

CHARLES A. - b. 1868, IN; s/o Cyrenus & Sarah A. (Jackson) Garlinghouse.

CHARLES A. - b. 20 Oct 1918, Chicago, Cook Co., IL; He served in World War II from 7 Dec 1941 to 20 Dec 1944 as Sergeant Major in 2nd Battalion Headquarters Company, 160th Infantry Regiment, 40th Division, US Army; s/o Walter S. & Eugenia "Jennie" (Meisel) Garlinghouse, Jr. m. Wilhelmine "Wilma" Emilie (Menzen) 16 Oct 1944, Detroit, MI, children Gail Wilma and Janet Elizabeth.

CHARLES OLIVER - b. 24 Jan 1855, IN; s/o George Bennett & Isabella Jolly (DeWitt) Garlinghouse. m. Minnie B. (Baskwell) 23 Sep 1877, Spencer Co., IN.

CHARLES R. - b. 23 Aug 1923, Ellenville, New York; d. 16 Oct 1963, Ellenville, New York; He served in WW II in Company A, 79th Tank Battalion, US Army; s/o Ira David & Esther Anna (Reed) Garlinghouse. m., children Charlene and Charles R., Jr.

CHARLES R, JR. - s/o Charles R. Garlinghouse.

CHARLES "CHARLEY" W. - b. 1871, Madison, Jefferson Co., IN; He served under Captain Wood in Company B, 3rd Cavalry, US Army from 7 Nov 1895 to 6 Nov 1898. This period included service during the War with Spain; s/o John Francis Oscar & Josephine "Rose" Olive (McFadden) Garlinghouse. m. Katherine (Dillon).

CHARLOTTE - b. @ 1887, Aitkin Co., Minn; d. 28 Sep 1888, Aitkin Co., Minn; d/o Ulysses Grant & Gertrude (Harrison) Garlinghouse.

CHARLOTTE (Stone) - m. Ace Nelson Garlinghouse 7 Aug 1936, children Carol Jean, Sandra Lee and Christie Lynn.

CHARLY "CHARLES" ABRAM - b. Sep 1871, Kan or Homer, Mich; d. 1934, Calhoun Co., Mich; Buried in Fairview Cem., Homer, MI. s/o Abraham "Abram" & Agnes A. (Rose) Garlinghouse. m. Louise (Hess) 20 Sep 1892, Calhoun Co., Mich, children Bryan Hess and Viola L.

CHLOE REBECCA (Beardsley) - b. 4 Jun 1836, Westmoreland, Oneida Co., NY; d. 11 May 1912, Clinton, Oneida Co., NY; Buried in Sunset Hill Cem., Clinton, NY. m. Joseph Garlinghouse, Jr. 4 Feb 1869, St. James Ch., Clinton, NY, children Anna Louise and John Newton. Chloe Rebecca taught school in Virginia in 1855 and later spent three years teaching in Georgia. After her husband Joseph died, in 1876, she conducted a private school in Clinton, NY.

CHRIS - b. 24 Jul 1956; d. 1 Feb 1992, Naples, FL; s/o Eugene Wayne & Bonnie (Crumback) Garlinghouse.

CHRISTIE LYNN - b. 21 Jun 1951; d/o Ace Nelson & Charlotte (Stone) Garlinghouse. m. Gregory Sauliere 29 Jan 1971.

CHRISTOPHER - s/o (...) & Tracy Lynn Garlinghouse (...). Living at Montverde, FL in 1996.

CHRISTOPHER THOMAS - b. 31 Dec 1987, CA; s/o William John & Judy (Glascock) Garlinghouse.

CHUCK W. - m. Marylen (...). Living at Richland, WA in 1996.

CINDY - d/o Vernon & Marie (Parker) Garlinghouse.

C.J. - Living at Brutus, MI in 1996.

CLARA "CARRIE" - b. 1887, Ft. Clark, TX; d.

1914-15, San Antonio, TX; d/o Walter S. & Julia Annie (Alder) Fisk Garlinghouse. m. Julius R. Prochnow 26 Jun 1905, San Antonio, TX, one child Fred.

CLARISSA MAYE - b. 9 May 1881, Raisin Twp., Lenawee Co., Mich; d. 6 Oct 1947, Detroit, Mich; d/o Gurdon Benedict & Minnie Minerva (Gates) Garlinghouse. m. Halleck Edward Wilson 23 Jun 1909, Tecumseh, Lenawee Co., Mich, children Virginia Edith and Douglas Garlinghouse.

CLYDE S. - b. 1876 Chautaqua Co., KS; s/o George C. & Hellin (Salisbury) Garlinghouse.

COLINA - b. 1 Dec 1851, Vernon, NJ; d/o John & Catherine Elizabeth (Utter) Garlinghouse.

COLLEEN (...) - m. ... Garlinghouse. Living at Missoula, MT in 1996.

COLLEEN JOANNE - b. 1965, Aitkin, Minn; d/o Robert Erwin & Agnes (Oakland) Garlinghouse.

CONNIE (Kreuger) - m. Randy Garlinghouse, one child Randy L., Jr.

CONNIE JEAN - b. 10 Jan 1962, Sault Ste. Marie, Mich; d/o Jerry Louis & Ruby Mary (Long) Garlinghouse.

CONSUELO HILDA (Ramerz) - m. Ralph Basil Garlinghouse 1952, children Elton Julian, Linda Mae, Brenda Jean and Deanana Lynn.

CORA (Oursler) - b. 16 Jun 1883; d. 21 Oct 1910; m. George Lovette Garlinghouse 30 May 1907, one child Matilda Cecile.

CORA BELL (Johnson) - b. 1858; d. 4 Mar 1922, Newark, NJ; m. Joseph Garlinghose 22 Sep 1886, Newark, NJ, children Ida B. and Sarah C.

CORA M. (Cockburn) - b. 12 Jun 1883, Jackson, Mich; d. 4 Oct 1968, Ann Arbor, Mich; Buried in Woodmere Cem., Detroit, Mich. m. Frank W. Garlinghouse 23 Oct 1902, Ann Arbor, Mich.

CORRINE (Sheldon) - m. Burton A. Garlinghouse 1941.

CYNTHIA - d/o Lacy & Elizabeth (McCormick) Garlinghouse. m. ... Grindle

CYNTHIA A. - b. 3 Apr 1820, Hart Co., KY; d. 15 Apr 1906, Ohio; d/o Gamaliel & Esther (Belknap) Garlinghouse. m. Franklin Gilbert, Licking Co., Ohio, children Sireno and Orin. m2nd. F. Christopher Avery.

CYNTHIA A. - b. 15 Oct 1877-78; d/o Jasper Sylvester & Rhoda Harriet (DuPey). m. David Grindle. m2nd. (...) Chase.

CYNTHIA ANN - b. 1956; d/o Loren Ira & Patricia Ann (Spaulding) Garlinghouse. m. Jerome Joseph McFarland 1973, one child Jason Michael.

CYNTHIA EMILY - b. 1846-48, Licking Co., Ohio; d. 28 April 1915, Plainfield, Hendricks Co., IN; d/o George & Sophronia (Sherman) Garlinghouse. m. Isaac Newton Inskeep 4 May 1865, children Emma Lulu, Albert, Maude, Grace, Clyde and Ralph.

CYRENUS A. - b. 5 Sep 1835, Switzerland Co., IN; d. 25 Nov 1912, Montezuma, IN; He served in the Civil War from 23 Sep 1861 to 31 Oct 1862 as Blacksmith (Private) in Company E, 50th Regiment, Indiana Infantry; s/o Cyrus Buell & Cassiah "Keziah" (Nichols) Garlinghouse. m. Sarah A. (Jackson) 1 Nov 1857, Ewington, IL, children Sylvester R., Eliza May, Alice "Allie", Franklin, Charles A., James, Jessie E., Lydia "Lidda", Odillie "Della" and Evaline M.

CYRIL - b. Apr 1887, Wash; s/o Norman Fayette "Frank" & Ada (...) Garlinghouse.

CYRUS BUELL, SR. - b. 1811-12, Ontario Co., New York; d. 22 Sep 1884, IN; s/o John G. & Lewanna (Bennett) Garlinghouse. m. Cassiah "Keziah" (Nichols) 21 Oct 1832, Clinton, IN, children Cyrenus A., John G., Martin V., Cyrus Buell, Jr., Lewana "Lovina", Evaline J. and Mariah "Maria" M.

CYRUS BUELL, JR. - b. 14 Aug 1843, Van Buren, Iowa; d. 15 Nov 1935, Crowell, TX; He served during the Civil War from 23 Sep 1861 to 10 Sep 1865 as private in Company E, 50th Regiment and 52nd Regiment, Indiana Infantry; s/o Cyrus Buell & Cassiah (Nichols) Garlinghouse. m. Amelia Florence (Fitzpatrick) 31 Apr 1879.

CYRUS BUELL, 3RD - b. 15 Oct 1879, Globe, Ariz; d. 1949, Globe, Ariz; s/o Martin V. & Sarah Ann (Long) Garlinghouse. m. Minnie (Lee) about 1915, one child William L.

D. (...) - m. Kevin Garlinghouse. Living at Sault St. Marie, MI in 1996.

D. - Living at Pasadena, CA in 1996.

D. - Living at Alhambra, CA in 1996.

D. - Living at Shawnee Mission, KS in 1996.

DAISY (...) - m. Ralph B. Garlinghouse. Living at New Baltimore, MI in 1996.

DAISY (...) m. Oscar Garlinghouse. Living at Fortuna, CA in 1996.

DALE - s/o ... Garlinghouse. m. Anna (...). Living at jacksonville, FL in 1996.

DALE LEE - b. 17 Jan 1953, Cedar Rapids, IA; s/o Edwin Oscar & Betsy Jean (Anderson) Garlinghouse.

DAN - Living at Paris Crossing, IN.

DANIEL BENJAMIN - b. 26 Nov 1817, Sussex Co., NJ; d. 22 Mar 1879, Wayne, Steuben Co., New York; s/o Thomas & Polly (Benjamin) Garlinghouse. m. Mary (Margeson) 27 Sep 1848, children Frank, Isaac Ashton and Mary Elizabeth. m2nd. Sarah "Sally" (Margeson), children Evaleen, Thomas Edison, Julia Ann, Grant, Alice Brundage and Polly.

DANIEL BENJAMIN - b. Jun 1842, Mich; d. 7 Oct 1931, Tecumseh, Mich; s/o David & Margaret Jane (Coryell) Garlinghouse. m. Carrie (Wolcott) B/4 1873, children Lulu E. and Edna M.

DARIUS HILL - b. 1 Nov 1833, Ontario Co., New York; d. 9 Nov 1896, Sand Springs, Iowa; He served in the Civil War from 17 Aug 1861 to 17 Oct 1862 as 1st Sergeant, Company I, 2nd Regiment, Iowa Cavalry. His commanding officer was Captain Washburn. s/o Samuel S. & Orpha (Harrington) Garlinghouse. m. Minerva Jane "Jennie" (White), children Jennie May, Emma Frank, Edmund Oscar, Almond Jewett, Lyman Edwin, Nelson Darius, Orpha Marie, Samuel Dayton, Jesse Mabel and Nina Grace.

DARLENE (...) - m. Don Garlinghouse. Living at Sault Ste. Marie, MI in 1996.

DARLENE LOUISE - b. 1954; d/o Ray Alden & Donna Annalee (Hausler) Garlinghouse. m. William Ficek 1975, children Steven Thomas and Shyla Marie.

DARWIN - b.

1957; s/o Ray Alden & Donna Annalee (Hausler) Garlinghouse.

DASIE L. - b. Jun 1893, Kan; d/o Fred W. & Flora J. (...) Garlinghouse.

DAVID - b. 10 Mar 1805, Sussex Co., NJ; d. 2 Jun 1897, Napoleon, Mich; s/o Thomas & Polly "Mary" (Benjamin) Garlinghouse. m. Margaret Jane (Coryell) 1831, Steuben Co., New York, children Ira Reed, John Coryell, Daniel Benjamin, Lettie "Violetta" and a daughter who died in infancy. m2nd. Mary Jane (Wilson) 16 Oct 1867, Somerset, Mich.

DAVID, JR. - b. 1855-56, Wapello Co., Iowa; s/o David Woodruff & Catherine (Garlinghouse) Garlinghouse. m. Sara (...) @ 1874, one child Evelyn. m2nd. Ella Jane (DuPey) 1 Nov 1876, Wyanett, Isanti Co., Minn.

DAVID B. - b. 18 Jun 1825, Vernon, NJ; d. 22

Oct 1899, Greenwood Lake, Orange Co., New York; s/o Gamaliel & Mary (Monroe) Garlinghouse, children James, Lucy and Georgiana.

DAVID BRYAN, SR. - b. 13 Jan 1901, Sussex Co., NJ; d. Jul 1964, NJ; s/o Sherwood Benjamin & Elizabeth (DeGraw) Garlinghouse. m. Ethel (Card), children David Bryan, Jr. and Herbert Hoover.

DAVID BRYAN, JR. - b. 15 Dec 1926, Sussex Co., NJ; d. 7 May 1975; s/o David Bryan & Ethel (Card) Garlinghouse. m. Hilda (Goetz) Moini.

DAVID CLARKE - b. 11 Jun 1947; d. 11 Nov 1963; s/o Wendell Lewis & Ella Helen (Skadeen) Garlinghouse.

DAVID J. Living at Miami, AZ, in 1996.

DAVID M. - Living at Ellenville, NY in 1996

DAVID ROYAL - b. 1953; s/o Royal Edsel & Kathryn (Blanchard) Garlinghouse.

DAVID WOODRUFF - b. 1810, Ontario Co., New York; d. 16 Jan 1881, Milaca, Minn; s/o John G. & Lewanna (Bennett) Garlinghouse. m. Grace (Mitchell) 31 Jan 1839, IN, children Lovina "Savina" and Mary Jane. m2nd. Catherine (Garlinghouse) 5 Jul 1849, Wapello Co., Iowa, children Jasper Sylvester, Lucretia D., David, Jr., Olive, Ulysses Grant, William Josiah, Sherman and Evelyn "Eva" "Evalina".

DAVIE L. - b. Jun 1893, Kan; d/o Fred W. & Flora J. (...) Garlinghouse.

DAWN (...) - m. Timothy Garlinghouse. One child Tim.

DAWN JANE - b. 1858, Ohio; d/o George & Sophronia (Sherman) Garlinghouse.

DEAN GEORGE - b. 19 Sep 1958, Sault Ste. Marie, Mich; s/o Lacy Grant & Ruby Ella (Colwell) Garlinghouse. m. M. (...). Living at Sault Ste. Marie, MI in 1996.

DEANANA LYNN - b. 1957; d/o Ralph Basil & Consuelo Hilda (Ramerz) Garlinghouse.

DEBBIE - d/o Vernon & Marie (Parker) Garlinghouse.

DEBORAH - b. @ 1778; possible d/o Stephen Gardenhouse (sic). She was niece of Kiziah Simmonsen of Warwick, Orange Co., NY, who died in 1796.

DEBORAH SUE - b. 20 Feb 1961, Sault Ste. Marie, Mich; d/o Frederick Mark & Doris Margaret (Long) Garlinghouse.

DEBRA LYNN - b. 1953; d/o Lyle Rapheil & Elizabeth (Cemer) Garlinghouse.

DELMAR - b. 31 Aug 1921: s/o Monroe and Grace (Shoemaker) Garlinghouse. m. Lynn /Evelyn (Sargent). One child Lyle David. m2nd Ruth (...)

DELORIS PATRICIA (Shotts) - m. Sherman Grant Garlinghouse, children Lester David and William Harry.

DELZELL (...) - m. Fred Bartlett Garlinghouse. One child Frederick Samuel.

DIANA (Morgan) - m. Robert Bruce Garlinghouse 4 Feb 1984, children Kathrine Marie Morgan and Allison Kabler.

DIANE ELIZABETH - d/o Mark & Elizabeth Victoria (Pope) Garlinghouse.

DIANE LYNN (Bernard) - b. 10 Apr 1946, Chicago, Cook Co., IL; m. Lester David Garlinghouse, children Jennifer Lynn and Kimberly Ann.

DIANE RUSSELL - b. 1967, Ellenville, NY; d/o Edward Joseph & Jane (Russell) Garlinghouse. m. Russell Guenste 1986, they have two sons.

DICK - s/o Richard & Eldora (...) Garlinghouse. Living at Lewiston, ID.

DOLLY - b. @ 1879; d. young; d/o Jasper Sylvester & Rhoda Harriet (DuPey) Garlinghouse.

DON - s/o ... Garlinghouse. m. Darlene (...). Living at Sault Ste Marie, MI in 1996.

DONALD -Living at Sault Ste Marie, MI in 1996.

DONALD - s/o ... Garlinghouse. Living at Mission, TX in 1996.

DONALD - b. 2 Jan 1926, Lewiston, Idaho; d. 24 Oct 1989, Coeur D'Alene, Idaho; s/o Gerald Arza & Elizabeth (Gilbert) Garlinghouse. Children two daughters.

DONALD - s/o Mark & Elizabeth Victoria (Pope) Garlinghouse.

DONALD - m. P. (...). Living at Marysville, OH in 1996.

DONALD ALBERT - b. 31 Dec 1923; s/o Harold Charles Garlinghouse.

DONALD L. - b. Delaware Co., Ohio; s/o Mervyn W. "Bud" & Grace (...) Garlinghouse. m. JoAnn B. (Nicol) 11 Jan 1957, children Tammi, Terri and Timothy.

DONNA MARIE (Schwieter) - b. 3 Jul 1958, Cincinnati, OH. m. Walter Sheldon Garlinghouse III at Knoxville, Tenn children Kevin Michael and John Edward.

DONNA (Falk) - b. Buena Park, CA; m. Kent Armin

Garlinghouse Aug 1967, one child Matthew Aaron.

DONNA ANNALEE (Hausler) -m. Ray Alden Garlinghouse 1953, children Darlene Louise, Darwin, Joyce and Michael.

DONNA R. (...) m. Kent Garlinghouse.Living at Alexandria, Minn in 1996.

DONNA RUBY - b. 15 Aug 1960, Sault Ste. Marie, Mich; d/o Jerry Louis & Ruby Mary (Long) Garlinghouse.

DORA (Harrison) - m. Ulysses Grant Garlinghouse, Aitkin Co., Minn.

DORA (Reyna) - b. 6 Jan 1931, Dominican Republic; d. Jul 1983, Dominican Republic; m. ... Campillo, one child Dorita. m2nd. Arthur Alder Garlinghouse, Orlando, FL, one child Walter Sheldon, III.

DORA E. - b. 24 Aug 1904, Lebanon, Montezuma, Colo; d/o Elias Buell & Virda Ellen (Lucas) Garlinghouse. m. Wesley Lee 13 Apr 1921, children Ada, Stanley, Delbert, Edith and Elsie.

DORA MAUDE - b. 1 Oct 1874, Hutchinson, Reno Co., Kan; d/o Lewis N. & Nancy Jane "Jennie" (Lockerman) Garlinghouse. m. Richard Alexander Tigner before 3 June 1898.

DORIS C. (...) - m. Harold James Garlinghouse 1960.

DORIS MARGARET (Long) - b. 27 Apr 1942, Sault Ste . Marie, Mich; m. Frederick Mark Garlinghouse 24 Jun 1960, Sault Ste., Marie, Mich, children Deborah Sue, Barbara Jean, Kathy Ann, Mark Samuel and Luke John.

DOROTHY - d/o John Ulmont & Eva Elizabeth (...)

Garlinghouse. m. ... Peron, one child Gene.

DOROTHY JEAN (Christian) - m. Earl Alonzo Garlinghouse 4 Jun 1954.

DOROTHY LILLIAN (Roessell) - b. 1915, Hillsborough, Kan; m. Morse Nolan Garlinghouse, children Jon Jay and Sandra.

DOROTHY MARGARET - b. 1910; d/o Sherman & Ella (...) Garlinghouse. m. Lawrence Frank.

DOROTHY (Rogers) - b. 17 Sep 1915; m. George L. Garlinghouse 26 Jan 1934, children John Newton and Norma Kay.

DWAYNE GRANT - b. 6 Oct 1943, Sault Ste. Marie, Mich; s/o Lacy Grant & Ruby Ella (Colwell) Garlinghouse

E. - s/o ... Garlinghouse. Living at Brea, CA in 1996.

EARL - b. Nov 1899, Kinross, Chippewa Co., Mich; d. at one year, Kinross, Chippewa Co., Mich; s/o Ulysses Grant Garlinghouse.

EARL - b. 17 May 1913, Hillsdale, Vermillion Co., IN; d. 1933, Hillsdale, Vermillion Co., IN; s/o LeRoy & Mary Ada (Ponton) Garlinghouse. m. Juanita (...).

EARL ALONZO - b. 20 Oct 1933; s/o Carroll & Velma Mae (Shirkey) Garlinghouse. m. Dorothy Jean (Christian) 4 Jun 1954.

EARL LEO - b. 13 Oct 1887, Galena, Delaware Co., Ohio; d. Dec 1974, Warner Robins, GA; Buried at Sunbury, Delaware Co., Ohio. s/o William E. & Luella (Crego) Garlinghouse. m. Oral C. (Whitney) 11 Nov 1908, Delaware Co., Ohio, children Leland, Mervyn W. "Bud" and Mildred. m2nd. Jeannette M. (Pyme) 12 Oct 1926, Delaware Co., Ohio, one child.

EARVEN - b. 2 Sep 1908, Aitkin Co., Minn; d. Sep 1978, Olympia, Wash; s/o William Josiah & Elizabeth Howe (Campbell). m. Ruby Ellen (Row).

EARVEN - m. Kathy (...). Living at Shelton, WA.

EDITH - b. Jan 1892, Kinross, Chippewa Co., Mich; d. 1957; d/o Ulysses Grant Garlinghouse. m. Bill Campbell, children Hazel and one other.

EDITH (Geiss) - b. 3 Dec 1888, NJ; d. Aug 1980, Vernon, Sussex Co., NJ; m. Sherwood Benjamin

Garlinghouse.

EDITH ESMA - b. 1912; d. 1970; d/o Edward Sylvester & Emma (Shae) Garlinghouse. m. Elmer Lunce, children Robert, David, Margaret, Donald, Ruth Ellen, Mary and Ann Louise

EDMUND OSCAR - b. 12 Jan 1867, Marshalltown, Iowa; d. 22 Apr 1934, Simms, Mont; s/o Darius Hill & Minerva Jane "Jennie" (White) Garlinghouse. m. Sarah (Wilson) 10 Jan 1894, children Oscar Ross, Hallie J. and Ralph Edwin. m2nd. Elizabeth Jane Allen (Bruce), children Alvin Nathan, Bruce Edmund and Edsie.

EDNA - b. 1878, IN; d/o Levi Curtis & Eva (Stuart) Garlinghouse.

EDNA M. - b. 1 Oct 1884-5, Tecumseh, Lenawee Co., Mich; d/o Daniel Benjamin & Carrie (Wolcott) Garlinghouse. m. ... Hill after 1918.

EDSIE -d/o Edmund Oscar & Elizabeth Jane Allen (Bruce) Garlinghouse.

EDWARD - b. 1972, Ellenville, Ulster Co., NY; s/o Edward Joseph & Jane (Russell) Garlinghouse.

EDWARD BUELL - b. 17 Jul 1936, Lewis, Montezuma Co., Colo; d. 31 Dec 1937, Los Angeles, CA; Buried at Lewis, Colo. s/o James Buell & Ruth (Huckabay) Garlinghouse.

EDWARD E. - d. Sep 1913; s/o ... Garlinghouse. m. Rose Edith (Justice) 14 Oct 1909, Tippecanoe Co., IN, one child Edward H. C.

EDWARD H. C. - b. 16 Jun 1910; s/o Edward E. & Rose Edith (Justice) Garlinghouse.

EDWARD JOSEPH - b. 6 Feb 1947, Ellenville,

Ulster Co., NY; d. 24 Sep 1992, W. Palm Beach, Palm Beach Co., FL; Buried in Sara Simms Memorial Gardens, Boynton Beach, FL. s/o Harold James & Catherine Maude (Spence) Garlinghouse, Sr. m. Jane (Russell) 21 Oct 1967, Ellenville, Ulster Co., NY, children Diane Russell, William and Edward. m2nd Lola Martens.

EDWARD SYLVESTER - b. 3 Sep 1880, Excelsior, Hennepin Co., Minn; d. 13 May 1943, Aitkin Co., Minn; s/o Jasper Sylvester & Rhoda Harriet (DuPey) Garlinghouse. m. Emma (Shae) 7 Nov 1908, children Raymond, Albert Edward, Edith Esma, Margaret, Eileen Edna, Robert Erwin, Thomas Grant, Owen Lee, Jeannette Madge and Patricia Eloise

EDWIN OSCAR - b. 1927; s/o Oscar Ross & Margaret (Hammer) Garlinghouse. m. Betsy Jean (Anderson) 27 Apr 1946, children Peter Lynn, Dale Lee and Paul Ray.

EFFIE GERTRUDE (Perrine) - b. 10 Nov 1869; d. 1915; m. John Edward Garlinghouse 20 Nov 1895, children Ira Burchfield, John Raymond, Elton Ellsworth and Vernon Lloyd.

EILEEN EDNA - b. 23 Sep 1915; d/o Edward Sylvester & Emma (Shae) Garlinghouse. m. Cecil Bergstrom, children Deanna and Beverly.

ELANOR "ELEANOR" (Hunt) - b. 4 May 1769, NJ; d. 31 Jul 1856, Van Buren Co., Iowa; She is buried in White Chapel Cem., Lick Creek Twp., Van Buren Co., Iowa. m. James Garlinghouse, children Catherine, Mary Ann, Jane, Gamaliel, Hannah, George, Rachel, Silas, Martha "Patty" and Eleanor.

ELBANNIS CARROLL - b. 12 Mar 1869, Ohio; d. 5 Feb 1953; s/o Lucian Bonaparte & Matilda Ruth (Hanawalt) Garlinghouse. m. Axie "Achsa" Mable (Yingling) 11 Nov 1891, children

Mildred and Carroll G.

ELCY LEE (Drury) - b. 17 Jun 1807, New York; d. 9 Jan 1892, Blakesburg, Iowa; m. George Garlinghouse 30 Dec 1824, Hardin Co., KY, children Hannah, James H.(M.), Elinor J., Silas, Isaac, Martha E., Gamaliel, Sarah A., Francis E., Letitia "Latitia", Melissa A. and John Andrew.

ELDORA (...) - m. Richard Garlinghouse one child Dick. Living at Lewiston, ID in 1996.

ELEANOR (...) - m. Richard Garlinghouse. Living at Colorado Springs, CO in 1996.

ELEANOR "Elena" - d/o James & Elanor "Eleanor" (Hunt) Garlinghouse. m. Thomas Robbins 21 Feb 1839, Franklin Co., Ohio, children Abraham, Harmen/Harmon, Rachel, Lafayette and Silas.

ELIAS BUELL. - b. 17 Nov 1868, Pueblo, Colo; d. 10 Dec 1931, Lewis, Montezuma, Colo; s/o Andrew Leonard & America J. (Bradburn) Garlinghouse. m. Virda Ellen (Lucas) 11 Nov 1901, Cortez, Colo., children Robert E., Nora, Dora E., Leonard, James Buell, Mary May, Benjamin Porter, Jennings Woodrow, Jennings Bryan, George William, Wallace Elias, Virda Marie, Martin LeRoy and Ruth Ethelene.

ELIAS M. - b. 1857, Van Buren, Iowa; s/o Andrew Leonard & Sarah Ann (Ratcliff) Garlinghouse.

ELINOR J. - b. 1830, Hart Co., KY; d/o George & Elcy Lee (Drury) Garlinghouse. m. J. B. Chapline 28 Feb 1854, KY.

ELIZA - b. 2 Nov 1819, NJ; d. 23 Sep 1898; d/o Joseph & Maria "Mary" (Ryerson) Garlinghouse. m. Isaac P. Haulenbeck B/4 1845, children Henry and Emma.

ELIZA (...) - b. PA; m. Henry Garlinghouse,

children Ellen J., Mary M., Lucy, James R., Ida Myrtle.

ELIZA (...) - m. Henry Garlinghouse, children Lacy and Ida.

ELIZA MAY - b. 1860; d/o Cyrenus A. & Sarah A. (Jackson) Garlinghouse. m. Zachary T. Benner 5 Sep 1878, Fountain Co., IN.

ELIZABETH "BETSY" - b. 15 Oct 1794; d. 17 Dec 1869, Richmond Ctr., New York; d/o John & Jane (Leonard) Garlinghouse. m. Victor Nelson Hopkins, children Socrates Nelson and Orville H.

ELIZABETH "BETSY" (Roberts) - b. 1800, New York; m. Stephen A. Garlinghouse 1824, children Hosita "Harriett", Lincina "Lucina", Elsmond, Samuel R. and Truman.

ELIZABETH (Huff) - b. 1831-32, Galena, Ohio; m. William Garlinghouse 1 Dec 1853, Delaware Co., Ohio, children Emerson, Mary F., George E., William E. and Reid.

ELIZABETH (McCormick) - b. 1836, Ohio; d. after 25 Sep 1916, Aitkin Co., Minn; m. Lacy Garlinghouse 18 Dec 1856, Blakesburg, Iowa, children Henry, Viola, Josiah, Ida, Rhoda, Cynthia and Esther A. m2nd. Otis W. Dodge 20 Sep 1881.

ELIZABETH (DeGraw) - b. 10 Jun 1880, Oakridge, NJ; d. 10 Jul 1905, Vernon, Sussex Co., NJ; m. Sherwood Benjamin Garlinghouse 9 Sep 1900, children David Bryan and John J.

ELIZABETH (Gilbert) - m. Gerald Arza Garlinghouse 1904, Kan, children Gerald Gilbert, Audrey, Rena, Marjie, Morse Nolan and Donald.

ELIZABETH (...) - m. Henry Garlinghouse, children Lacy and Ida.

ELIZABETH (Cemer) - m. Lyle Rapheil Garlinghouse 1944, children Laura Ann, Debra Lynn and Penny Sue.

ELIZABETH AMY WESTFALL (Soults) - b. 6 Mar 1917, Eugene, Oregon; m. Leslie Holmes Garlinghouse, Jr., children Leslie Homer, Roland Edgar and Susan Lee.

ELIZABETH CLARK - b. 8 Jan 1978; d/o Richard Earl, Jr. & Margaret Ann (Pettys) Garlinghouse.

ELIZABETH E. (...) - b. 1844; d. 1939, Switzerland Co., IN; Buried in Vevay, Switzerland Co., IN. m. ... Garlinghouse. m2nd. Manuel Forewood 26 Dec 1864, Switzerland Co., IN, one child Viola.

ELIZABETH HAYES (Davison) - b. 1890, Minot, ND; m. Ralph Leman Garlinghouse 15 Nov 1919, Fresno, CA, children Nancy Elizabeth, Ralph Spalding and Grant Wesley.

ELIZABETH HOWE (Campbell) - b. 9 May 1884, Kalamazoo, Mich; d. 1959, Tacoma, Wash; m. William Josiah Garlinghouse 1900, children James Rufus, twins Frank and Frances, Earven, Bessie, Ella Mae, Bud and Sherman Grant.

ELIZABETH JANE ALLEN (Bruce) - b. Marshalltown, Iowa; d. 30 Aug 1940, Simms, Mont; m. Edmund Oscar Garlinghouse 1908, children Bruce Edmund and Edsie.

ELIZABETH VICTORIA (Pope) - b. 9 Jul 1916; m. Mark Garlinghouse 11 Apr 1933, Sault Ste. Marie, Mich, children Frederick Mark, Jerry Louis, Donald, Diane Elizabeth, Leon, Bradley Gene and Randy John. m2nd. (...) Jones.

ELLA (Orahood) - d. B/4 21 Feb 1883; m. Sylvester R. Garlinghouse 6 Aug 1879, Fountain Co., IN

ELLA (...) - m. Sherman Garlinghouse, children Dorothy and Irene May.
ELLA (Davis) - m. Frank Garlinghouse.

ELLA HELEN (Skadeen) - d. 7 Jan 1951; m. Wendell Lewis Garlinghouse 16 Mar 1940, children Anne Patricia and David Clarke.

ELLA JANE (DuPey) - b. @ 1861, Mich; d. 22 Mar 1898, Minn; m. David Garlinghouse, Jr. 1 Nov 1876, Isanti Co., Minn.

ELLA MAE - b. 9 Mar 1917, Aitkin Co., Minn; d. 1968; d/o William Josiah & Elizabeth Howe (Campbell) Garlinghouse. m. Clifford Hodge.

ELLA MURAT - b. 9 Jul 1894, Madison, Jefferson Co., IN; d. Prob. May 1971; d/o Willard Elmer & Mary Elizabeth (Ashley) Garlinghouse. m. Fred DeArmond.

ELLEN - b. 16 Dec 1826, NJ; d/o Joseph & Maria "Mary" (Ryerson) Garlinghouse. m. Stephen Wood 23 Feb 1846, Newark, NJ, children Georgeanna, Stephen and William.

ELLEN - b. 6 Jan 1828, Richmond, New York; d. 2 Dec 1868, LeRoy, New York; d/o Joseph & Submit (Sheldon) Garlinghouse. m. Maj. Horatio G. Sheldon 14 Apr 1866, LeRoy, NY

ELLEN (Courter) - b. 1858, IN; m. ... Downey. m2nd. Charles Garlinghouse 19 Nov 1884, Switzerland Co., IN.

ELLEN (Landers) - m. Levi Curtis Garlinghouse 16 Mar 1899, Jefferson Co., IN.

ELLEN (Ekman) - b. Batavia, IL; m. Ralph Spalding Garlinghouse 1951, Batavia, IL, children Bruce, Ann, John Spalding and Philip.

ELLEN J. - b. 1867, Minn; d/o Henry & Eliza

(...) Garlinghouse.

ELLEN JANE - b. 22 Sep 1942; d/o Lester Edwin & Gladys Grace (Taylor) Garlinghouse. m. Robert J. Rainey 27 Dec 1962, children Jess Edwin, and twins Janelle Jane and Jeanette Jane.

ELMER BUELL - b. 30 Jan 1895, Crowell, Foard Co., TX; d. Aug 1968, Baldwin Pk., CA; s/o Cyrus Buell, Jr. & Amelia Florence (Fitzpatrick) Garlinghouse.

ELMER GEORGE - b. 17 Aug 1904; d. 1924; s/o Samuel Dayton & Belle (McBride) Garlinghouse.

ELNORA - d/o George B. & Josie (Robison) Garlinghouse.

ELOISE (...) - b. 7 Feb 1930; d. Feb 1982, Hoquiam, Wash; m. Bud Garlinghouse.

ELSA G. - b. Sep 1879, Iowa; d/o John Andrew & Laura M. (Vancleave) Garlinghouse.

ELSIE LEE (Armstrong) - b. May 1887-88, Beason, IL; d. 1945, Pasadena, CA; m. Leslie Holmes Garlinghouse Aug 1912, Canon City, Colo, children Leslie Holmes and Lucy Lee.

ELSIE SOPHIA (Heberger) - m. ... Chase. m2nd. Leonard Deal Garlinghouse 15 Apr 1936.

ELSMOND - b. 1830, New York; s/o Stephen A. & Elizabeth "Betsy" (Roberts) Garlinghouse.

ELTON ELLSWORTH - b. 20 Mar 1903; d. 23 Jul 1990, Hazel Pk., Mich; s/o John Edward & Effie Gertrude (Perrine) Garlinghouse. m. Leona (Beckman) 1923, children Junior Ellsworth, Lyle Rapheil, Royal Edsel, Ralph Basil and Barbara Leigh.

ELTON JULIAN - b. 1953; s/o Ralph Basil and Consuelo Hilda (Ramerz.

EMERSON - b. 10 Dec 1853; d. 23 Feb 1858, Van Buren Co., Iowa; Buried in White Chapel Cem., Lick Creek Twp., Van Buren Co., Iowa. s/o William and Elizabeth (Huff) Garlinghouse.

EMERY - b. 1841, Licking Co., Ohio; d. 2 Aug 1864, Atlanta, GA; Buried Centerville Cem., Harlem Twp., Delaware Co., Ohio. He served in the Civil War from 21 July 1861 to 2 Aug 1864 as Corporal in Company I, 32nd Regiment, Ohio Infantry. He died of gunshot wounds received in battle near Atlanta, Georgia. s/o George & Sophronia (Sherman) Garlinghouse.

EMILY - b. 17 Apr 1823, Hart Co., KY; d. 23 Dec 1897, Victor, Iowa Co., Iowa; d/o Gamaliel & Esther (Belknap) Garlinghouse. m. Isaiah Simpson 6 Jun 1842, Licking Co., Ohio, children George Irvin, Sarah Ann, Esther Ellen and Omer. Isaiah Simpson was 1st cousin to President U. S. Grant

EMILY S. (Baker) - b. 17 Aug 1841, Jerusalem, New York; d. 26 Oct 1934, Rochester, New York; m. Lyman Strowbridge 7 Jun 1865, children Frank L. and Fred. m2nd. Samuel R. Garlinghouse Jan 1876, children Eugene and Grace June. m3rd. John Powers. m4th. Barber Eldridge 21 Mar 1900, Naples, New York.

EMMA (Shae) - b. Swan River, Manitoba, Canada; d. Newcastle, Weston Co., Wyoming; m. Edward Sylvester Garlinghouse 7 Nov 1908, children Raymond, Albert Edward, Edith Esma, Margaret, Eileen Edna, Robert Erwin, Thomas Grant, Owen Lee, Jeannette Madge and Patricia Eloise.

EMMA (Card) - b. 1 Mar 1886; d. 27 Sep 1940, Sussex Co., NJ; Buried in North Church Cemetery, Hardyston, NJ; m. John Garlinghouse children James Amsey and Ida Belle.

EMMA FRANK - b. 21 Feb 1866, Worthington, Iowa; d. 29 Sep 1877, Worthington, Iowa; d/o Darius

Hill & Minerva Jane "Jennie" (White) Garlinghouse.

EMMA KATE - b. 7 Mar 1878, Kan; d/o Martin V. & Sarah Ann (Long) Garlinghouse. m. LeRoy Newberry.

EMMA L. - b. 9 Mar 1860, Allens Hill, New York; d. 9 Jan 1952, Allens Hill, New York; d/o John Nelson & Lucy West (Bothwell) Garlinghouse. m. Richard M. Allen @ 1903, one child Tracy.

EMMA PERMELIA (Sherman) - b. 12 Jun 1860, Belvedere, IL; d. 28 Nov 1942, Glendale, CA; m. Holmes Spalding Garlinghouse 16 Dec 1885, Leadville, Colo., children Sherman, Leslie Holmes, Ralph Leman and Albert Frederick.

ERIC - b. 1974, Atlanta, GA; s/o Richard G. Garlinghouse. Living at Acworth, GA in 1996.

ERLE - b. 1892, Indiana; s/o ... Garlinghouse. He was listed in the 1910 Census for Chicago, Cook Co., IL.

ESTELA (del Pozo) - m. Leslie Homer Garlinghouse 27 Sep 1964.

ESTHER (Belknap) - b. 1 Apr 1797, Middletown, Ontario Co., New York; d. 16 Feb 1879, Alexandria, Licking Co., Ohio; m. Gamaliel Garlinghouse 1812, Ontario Co., New York, children Cynthia A., George, Emily, Orin and Riley.

ESTHER (Jonsson) - b. 23 Aug 1901, Mich; d. Apr 1982, Amarillo, TX; m. Arthur Alder Garlinghouse, Jr., at Fayetteville, Ark.

ESTHER - d/o Ira David & Esther Anna (Reed) Garlinghouse. m. ... Lascalzo.

ESTHER A. - d/o Lacy & Elizabeth (McCormick) Garlinghouse. m. ... Bacon.

ESTHER ANNA (Reed) - b. 15 Mar 1890, Broome Center, NY; d. 1979, Ellenville, NY; m. Ira David Garlinghouse, children Esther, Harold James, Charles R. and Ira W.

ESTHER WINIFRED (Coghill) - b. 12 Aug 1907; d. Oct 1985, Rogers, Ark; m. Robert Orestes Garlinghouse, M.D., children Mary Jean and Jane Esther.

ETHA - b. 1869, Mich; d/o Ira Reed & Melissa A. (Coryell) Garlinghouse. m. Clayton Graham 8 Dec 1893.

ETHALINDA J. - b. 19 Jul 1808, Sussex Co., NJ; d. 17 Feb 1893, Pleasant Valley, Steuben Co., New York; d/o Thomas & Polly "Mary" (Benjamin) Garlinghouse. m. Ira "E.G." Read, children Rozilla, Phoebe Maria, Ellen J., Ann Eliza and Mary A.

ETHALYN VIRGINIA - b. 1882, Tecumseh, Lenawee Co., Mich; d. 1955; d/o Gurdon Benedict & Minnie Minerva (Gates) Garlinghouse.

ETHEL (...) - b. 2 Mar 1897; d. May 1977, Colorado Springs, Colo; m. ... Garlingh5use.

ETHEL (...) - b. 7 Oct 1898; d. Jul 1980, Mancos, Colo; m. ... Garlinghouse.

ETHEL (...) - b. 14 Jul 1898; d. Feb 1181, Dayton, Ohio; m. ... Garlinghouse.

ETHEL (...) - m. Richard Garlinghouse 1945.

ETHEL (Card) - d. 1963-65; m. David Bryan Garlinghouse, children David Bryan, Jr. and Herbert Hoover.

ETHEL - d/o Jeremiah "Gerald" Garlinghouse.

ETHEL (Cash) - m. Robert E. "Bob" Garlinghouse 1926.

ETHEL M. - b. 8 Mar 1896; d/o Franklin & Laura (Newman) Garlinghouse. m. John D. Sweeney 24 Jun 1913, Newport, Vermillion Co., IN.

ETHEL ROSE- b. 28 Apr 1892 Monroe Twp, Ohio; d. Sep 1971, Johnstown, Ohio; d/o George E. & Caroline "Callie" S. (Knorr) Garlinghouse.

EUGENE - b. 1871, New York; d. 1871, New York; Buried in Rose Ridge cem., Naples, New York. s/o Samuel R. & Emily S. (Baker) Garlinghouse.

EUGENE WAYNE - b. 1933; s/o Vernon Lloyd & Margaret Lillian (Kaufman) Garlinghouse. m. Bonnie (Crumback) 1953, children Sherie, Randy, Chris and Larry.

EUGENIA "JENNIE" (Meisel) - b. 23 Jan 1889, Chicago, Cook Co., IL; d. 23 Oct 1970, Chicago, Cook Co., IL; Buried in Ridgewood Cem., Cook Co., IL. m. Walter S. Garlinghouse, Jr., children Ferdinand Walter and Charles Albert.

EUNICE - d/o Reid & Sue E. "Lou" (Miller) Garlinghouse.

EVA (Stuart) - b. 1858, IN; m. Levi Curtis Garlinghouse 1 Aug 1876, children Alice, Irene and Edna.

EVA - d/o James & Anna (Bennet) Garlinghouse. m. ...Brinkman, children Edward and Lillian.

EVA (Mahoney) - b. 6 Oct 1930; m. Louis Edward Garlinghouse, one child Gail Elaine.

EVA "Elizabeth" (...). m. John Ulmont Garlinghouse, one child Dorothy.

EVA JEAN - b. 24 Mar 1902, Delaware Co., Ohio; d. 8 Mar 1903, Delaware Co., Ohio; Buried in the Carr Family Cem., Delaware Co., Ohio. d/o

Reid & Sue E. "Lou" (Miller) Garlinghouse.

EVA O. (Watson) - b. 16 Jan 1892, Hillsdale, Vermillion Co., IN; d. Hillsdale, IN; Buried in Helt's Prairie Cem., Vermillion Co., IN. m. Hugh A. Garlinghouse, children Herbert, Mangnia Elizabeth and Treva. m2nd. Earl Millikan.

EVALEEN - b. 28 Dec 1855, Wayne, Steuben Co., New York; d. 14 Jul 1861, Wayne, Steuben Co., New York; d/o Daniel Benjamin & Sarah "Sally" (Margeson) Garlinghouse.

EVALINA FLORENCE "FLORA" - b. 20 Aug 1876, Kan; d/o Martin V. & Sarah Ann (Long) Garlinghouse. m. ... Ikenberry, one child Flora.

EVALINE J. - b. 1849, Van Buren, Iowa; d/o Cyrus Buell & Cassiah "Keziah" (Nichols) Garlinghouse. m. George W. Martin 26 Dec 1866, Spencer Co., IN.

EVALINE M - b. Oct 1884, IN; d/o Cyrenus A. & Sarah A. (Jackson) Garlinghouse. m. Charles A. Patterson 3 Oct 1902, Vermillion Co., IN.

EVELYN "EVIA" - b. 1866, IL; d/o George C. & Hellin (Salisbury) Garlinghouse.

EVELYN "EVA" "EVALINA" - b. 10 Apr 1875, Mille Lacs, Minn; d/o David & Sara (...) Garlinghouse, Jr. m. Vern Grindle, one child David

FANNY (Shears) - b. Palestine, IL; m. Willard Elmer Garlinghouse @ 1880, one child Tilden Willard.

FANNY B. - b. 1867, Allens Hill, New York; d. 1959, Richmond, New York; She is buried in Lakeview Cemetery, Ontario Co., NY. d/o John Nelson & Lucy West (Bothwell) Garlinghouse. m. Frank Hoagland 18 May 1901, Ontario Co., New York. m2nd. George Pitts Reed.

FAYETTE - b. 1898, Kansas; s/o Sherman Fayette & Olive (Palmer) Garlinghouse. m. Lynn (Hartman) 28 Jan 1916.

FERDINAND WALTER - b. 1 Sep 1912, Chicago, I5; s/o Walter Sheldon, Jr. & Eugenia Jennie" (Meisel) Garlinghouse.

FERN E. (...) - b. 1889; m. Glenwood K. Garlinghouse.

FERN L. - b. 26 Oct 1907, Sand Springs, Iowa; d. 2 Apr 1912, Kansas City, Jackson Co., MO; Buried at Forest Hills Cem., Jackson Co., MO. d/o Samuel Dayton & Belle (McBride) Garlinghouse.

FERNE BEATRICE (Armstrong) - b. 2 Jul 1891, Beason, IL; d. May 1949, S. Pasadena, CA; m. Albert Frederick Garlinghouse Aug 1915, Canon City, Colo., children Margaret "Peggy" Lee and Albert Frederick.

FLORA - b. 1870; d. 1911; d/o Thomas & Susan (Osborne) Garlinghouse. m. Alfred Lacey.

FLORA J. (...) - b. Nov 1865, New York; m. Fred

W. Garlinghouse 1890, children Dasie L. and Fredie J.

FLORENCE (...) - b. 4 Jan 1907; d. Oct 1983, Flagstaff, Ariz; m. ... Garlinghouse.

FLORENCE (Schultz) - m. George William Garlinghouse 7 Nov 1942, children Linda, William "Bill," Terry and Jon.

FLORENCE A. "Florina" - b. Dec 1881-2, Ohio; d. 1931, Johnstown, Ohio; d/o George E. & Caroline S. "Callie" (Knorr) Garlinghouse. m. Ray Adams, one child Harry R.

FLORENCE LUANNA - b. 18 Sep 1892, Madison, Jefferson Co., IN; d. 4 Jan 1953, San Bernardino, CA; d/o Willard Elmer & Elizabeth (Ashley) Garlinghouse. m. Joseph Harding Weber 5 Oct 1910, Madison, IN, children Charles Willard and James Lanier. m2nd. Jesse Denmore Adams, Marietta, Ohio, children James Delray, Almeda May, John Wickersham, Dennis and Joseph Lanier.

FORESTE (Smith) - b. 17 Feb 1905, IN; d. May 1987, Madison, Jefferson Co., IN; M. Fred Bartlett Garlinghouse.

FRANCES (...) - b. 13 Mar 1890; d. Jul 1974, Breckenridge, Minn; m. ... Garlinghouse.

FRANCES L. - b. 28 Jul 1904, Aitkin Co., Minn; d/o William Josiah & Elizabeth Howe (Campbell) Garlinghouse. m. Pearl H. Nulf. She is twin of Frank.

FRANCES (DeVerter) - m. Herbert Garlinghouse.

FRANCESCO BRUCE - b. 21 Jul 1860, Jefferson Co., IN; d. 14 Mar 1863, Jefferson Co., IN; s/o George Bennett & Isabella Jolly (DeWitt) Garlinghouse.

FRANCIS E. - b. 1842, Hart Co., KY; s/o George

& Elcy Lee (Drury) Garlinghouse.

FRANCIS M. Bryan, Mrs. - m2nd. Gurdon Benedict Garlinghouse 1914, Tecumseh, Lenawee Co., Mich.

FRANCIS MARK - b. 4 Dec 1914, Topeka, Kan; d. 21 Dec 1982, New York, NY; s/o Lewis Fayette & Katherine (Fogwell) Garlinghouse. m. Marjorie Cosper (Beard) 18 Nov 1939, at 1st Methodist Church of Topeka, Kan., children Bradley Kent, Webb Mark and Whitney Beard.

FRANK - b. 7 Dec 1849, Wayne, Steuben Co., New York; d. 6 Mar 1852, Wayne, Steuben Co., New York; s/o Daniel Benjamin & Mary (Margeson) Garlinghouse.

FRANK - b. 5 Jun 1892, Delaware Co., Ohio; d. 15 Feb 1953, V.A. Hosp., Hines, Cook Co., IL; He served in World War I as private in the Meuse-Argonne AEF 1918-19. He was discharged 27 May 1919; s/o Reid & Sue E. "Lou" (Miller) Garlinghouse.

FRANK - b. 28 Jul 1904, Aitkin Co., Minn; d. 16 Oct 1973, Olympia, Wash; s/o William Josiah & Elizabeth Howe (Campbell) Garlinghouse. m. Ella (Davis). m.2nd Ruby (Doyle). He is twin of Frances L.

FRANK DEWEY - b. 23 Jun 1899, Sussex Co., NJ; d. 15 Mar 1976, Budd Lake, NJ; s/o John Monroe & Jesteen D. (Farber) Garlinghouse. m. Ruth (Pettinger) Jun 1925, one child Frank Dewey, Jr.

FRANK DEWEY, JR. -s/o Frank Dewey & Ruth (Pettinger) Garlinghouse.

FRANK W. - b. 14 Sep 1876, Romeo, Mich; d. 22 Apr 1939, Ann Arbor, Mich; He served in the Spanish-American War as Corporal in Co. A, 31st Regiment, Michigan Infantry from 26 Apr 1898 to 31 Mar 1899; s/o Nelson S. & Mary E.

(Willits) Garlinghouse. m. Cora M. (Cockburn) 23 Oct 1902, Ann Arbor, Mich.

FRANKLIN - b. 1866, IN; s/o Cyrenus A. & Sarah A. (Jackson) Garlinghouse. m. Harriet (White). m2nd. Laura (Newman), children Male, Ethyl Mary and a stillborn.

FRANKLIN BENNETT - b. 27 Nov 1873, IN; d. 12 Apr 1927; s/o Aurelius DeWitt & Mary "Mollie" (deBruler) Garlinghouse. m. Lilly M. (Grady) 27 Nov 1896, Spencer Co., IN, children Helen D., Aurelius DeWitt and Anna.

FRANKLIN R. - b. 1841, Richmond, New York; d. 1845, Richmond, New York; s/o Samuel S. & Orpha (Harrington) Garlinghouse.

FRED - Living at Barbeau, MI in 1996.

FRED - s/o ... Garlinghouse. Living at Pueblo, CO in 1996.

FRED BARTLETT - b. Oct 1897, IN; d. Jefferson Co., IN; He served in World War I. His name is included on WW I Memorial in Indianapolis, IN; s/o John Francis Oscar & Mary E. (McClure) Garlinghouse. m. ... (Delzell), one child Frederick Samuel. m2nd. Foreste (Smith).

FRED LEE - b. 5 Jun 1896, Arcade, New York; d. Oct 1964, New York; He served in the US Marine Corps during World War I; s/o Arthur L. & Sarah M. (Baker) Garlinghouse. m. Gertrude (Verheyen) 10 Jan 1919 or 9 Jun 1920.

FRED W. - b. Nov 1867, IL; s/o George C. & Hellen " Hellin" (Salisbury) Garlinghouse. m. Flora J. (...) 1890, children Dasie L. "Donna" and Fred W., Jr.

FRED W, Jr. - b. Feb 1895, Kan; d. 9 Oct 1918, aboard USS Solace; s/o Fred W. & Flora J.

(...) Garlinghouse. m. Rhoda F. (...). He died of pneumonia while serving in the US Navy during WW 1

FREDERICK - s/o Albert Edward & Lorraine (Fredericks) Garlinghouse.

FREDERICK L. - b. 21 Oct 1871, Bristol, New York; d. 13 Jan 1946, Brooklyn, New York; s/o Arthur L. & Carrie A. (Philips) Garlinghouse. m. Ida (Tomkins) 1891, one child Richard.

FREDERICK LEMAN - b. 19 Aug 1849, Littleville, New York; d. 11 Feb 1940, Glenshaw, PA; s/o Leman Benton & Martha Ann (Spalding) Garlinghouse. m. Mary Ellen (Gilpatrick) 3 Apr 1878, Saco, ME, one child Nanie.

FREDERICK MARK - b. 20 Feb 1934, Sault Ste. Marie, Mich; s/o Mark & Elizabeth Victoria (Pope) Garlinghouse. m. Doris Margaret (Long) 24 Jun 1960, Sault Ste. Marie, Mich, children Deborah Sue, Barbara Jean, Kathy Ann, Mark Samuel and Luke John.

FREDERICK PAUL - b. 30 Jun 1907, Delaware Co., Ohio d. 10 Sep 1907, Delaware Co., Ohio; s/o Reid & Sue E. "Lou" (Miller) Garlinghouse.

FREDERICK "RICKY" MYERS - b. Sep 1962, Pasadena, CA; s/o Albert Frederick & Barbara Evlyn (Myers) Garlinghouse.

FREDERICK SAMUEL - b. 26 Jun 1936, IN; s/o Fred Bartlett & ...(Delzell) Garlinghouse. m. Marie (...).

FREDERICKA (...) - m. Richard G. Garlinghouse. one child Eric.

G. (...) - m. ... Garlinghouse. Living at Torrance, CA in 1996.

G. - s/o ... Garlinghouse. Living at Oakland, CA in 1996.

G. K. - s/o ... Garlinghouse. m. Georgia Ann (Johnson).

G W. - b. 1880, Ariz; d. B/4 13 Apr 1898; s/o Martin V. & Sarah Ann (Long) Garlinghouse.

GAIL ELAINE - b. 5 Aug 1949; d/o Louis Edward & Eva (Mahoney) Garlinghouse.

GAIL WILMA - b. 21 Feb 1946, Evanston, IL; d/o Charles A. & Wilhelmine "Wilma" E. (Menzen) Garlinghouse. m. Ernest Norbert Rysso 4 May 1968, Chicago, IL, one child Jennifer Leigh.

GAMALIEL - b. 30 Jul 1776, Vernon, NJ; d. 1 Nov 1856, Vernon, NJ; Buried in the United Methodist Churchyard, Vernon, Sussex Co., NJ. s/o James & Johanna (Buchanan) Garlinghouse. m. Mary Monroe 1800, children Thomas, Mary, James, John, George, Hannah "Ma", Mary, David B. and Thomas D.

GAMALIEL - b. 26 Mar 1792, Luzerne Co., PA; d. 1873, Topeka, Kan; s/o James & Elanor "Eleanor" (Hunt) Garlinghouse. m. Esther (Belknap) 1812, Ontario Co., NY, children Cynthia A., George, Emily, Orin and Riley.

GAMALIEL - b. 30 May 1836, Hart Co., KY; d. 23 Feb 1856, Hart Co., KY; s/o George & Elcy Lee (Drury) Garlinghouse.

GARY - Living at Mason City, Iowa in 1996.

GARY GENE - b. 1947; s/o Junior Ellsworth & Lucy (Gascho) Garlinghouse.

GENEVIEVE E. (McClory). m. Lawrence Edwin Garlinghouse 23 May 1966, children Marie "Meg" E. and Lawrence Edwin.

GENEVIEVE MAY (Aldread) - b. 1904; m. John Raymond Garlinghouse 1926, children Phyllis Marguerite, Ray Alden and Carol.

GEORGE - b. 23 Oct 1800, Ontario Co., New York; d. 1 Jun 1865, Blakesburg, Iowa: s/o James & Elanor "Eleanor" (Hunt) Garlinghouse. m. Elcy Lee (Drury) 30 Dec 1824, Hardin Co., KY, children Hannah, James H.,Elinor J., Silas, Isaac, Martha E., Gamaliel, Sarah A., Francis E., Letitia "Latitia", Malissa A. and John Andrew.

GEORGE - b. 20 Aug 1816, Vernon, Sussex Co., NJ; d. 24 Mar 1869, Vernon, Sussex Co., NJ; s/o Gamaliel & Mary (Monroe) Garlinghouse. m. Amelia (Webb), Vernon, NJ, children Martha, Mary, Anna and Amelia "Aurilla" Orvilla.

GEORGE - b. 1817, Ontario Co., New York; d. 1890, Licking Co., Ohio; s/o Gamaliel & Esther (Belknap) Garlinghouse. m. Sophronia (Sherman). 10 Sep 1840, Licking Co., Ohio, children Emery, Lucian Bonaparte, Cynthia, Sherman Fayette, Dawn Jane and Riley.

GEORGE - b. 9 Jan 1844, Ohio; d. 17 Jan 1855, Delaware Co., Ohio; Buried in Fancher Rd. Cem., Delaware Co., Ohio. s/o Silas & Margaret (Reid) Garlinghouse.

GEORGE - b. 15 Aug 1856, Newark, NJ; d. 5 Sep 1856, Newark, NJ; s/o John & Sarah (Polhemus) Garlinghouse.

GEORGE ARZA - b. 1902, Kan; s/o Arthur Richard & Anna B. (Jones) Garlinghouse. One child

Anadella.

GEORGE B. - b. 5 Feb 1870, Pueblo, Colo; s/o Andrew Leonard & America J. (Bradburn) Garlinghouse. m. Josie (Robison) 18 Jan 1899, Montezuma, Colo, children Elenora, Wallace, Heggie and Vivian.

GEORGE BENNETT - b. 15 Nov 1815, Ontario Co., New York; d. 14 Apr 1885, Madison, IN; s/o John G. & Lewanna "Louanna" (Bennett) Garlinghouse. m. Isabella Jolly (DeWitt), children George Perry, Aurelius DeWitt, Paulina Jane, John Francis Oscar, Levi Curtis, Charles Oliver, Viola Mariah and Francesco Bruce. m2nd. Serena Milton Boyd (Crusan) 6 Jan 1864, IN, children Lorenzo Clay, Willard Elmer, Serena Luvada and Ulysses Arthur.

GEORGE C. - b. 1841-2, IN; s/o Benjamin & Catherine Maria (Williams) Garlinghouse. m. Hellin (Salisbury) 20 Jul 1863 at McDonough Co. IL, children Evelyn, Fred W., Opal, Clyde S. and Mavis.

GEORGE E. - b. 4 Jun 1858, Van Buren Co., Iowa; d. 1 Feb 1945, Johnstown, Delaware Co., OH; s/o William & Elizabeth (Huff) Garlinghouse. m. Caroline "Callie" S. (Knorr) 3 July 1877, Delaware Co., OH, children Florence "Florina" A., Glenwood K. and Ethel Rose. George E. imported the first draft mares from France. In 1901, he entered a yearling draft mare in the General Sweepstakes Class at the Ohio State Fair. The yearling won first prize, and subsequently won six other prizes.

GEORGE HOWARD - b. 9 May 1898, Madison, Jefferson Co., IN; d. 22 Apr 1950, IN; s/o Willard Elmer & Mary Elizabeth (Ashley) Garlinghouse. m. Margaret (Stephenson) 1918, one child Inez Florence. m2nd. Mildred Jones 23 Feb 1924, children George "Billy" Willard, Betty Jo, Louis Edward, Nathan Andrew, Nancy

Joyce, John Daniel and Lois Jane.

GEORGE L., JR. - b. 23 Oct 1915; d. May 1976; s/o George Lovette & Carrie Mae (Kingsbury) Garlinghouse. m. Dorothy (Rogers) 26 Jan 1934, children John Newton and Norma Kay.

GEORGE LOVETTE - b. 14 Jan 1875, Shawnee Co., Kan; d. Mar 1966, Colorado Springs, Colo; s/o Lucian Bonaparte & Matilda Ruth (Hanawalt) Garlinghouse. m. Cora (Oursler) 30 May 1907, children Matilda Cecile and George L. Jr. m2nd. Carrie Mae (Kingsbury). m3rd. Minnie L. (Divilbiss). m4th. Valerie (Johnson).

GEORGE M. - b. 1860, Effingham Co., IL; s/o Andrew Leonard & Sarah Ann (Ratcliff) Garlinghouse.

GEORGE M. - b., Iowa; s/o John Andrew & Laura M. (Vancleave) Garlinghouse.

GEORGE PERRY - b. 1 Nov 1841, Madison, Jefferson Co., IN; s/o George Bennett & Isabella Jolly (DeWitt) Garlinghouse. m. Sarah "Sally" E. (Cotton) 16 Mar 1864, Switzerland Co., IN, children William DeWitt, Hattie "Netta" and Viola.

GEORGE WILLARD "BILLY" - b. 21 Nov 1924, Madison, Jefferson Co., IN; d. May 1966; s/o George Howard & Mildred (Jones) Garlinghouse. m. Irene (Laird) 5 Feb 1946, Madison, IN.

GEORGE WILLIAM - b. 4 Feb 1917, Lebanon, Montezuma Co., Colo; d. 7 Nov 1987, Yuba, Placer Co., Colo; He served as Major in the US Air Corps in World War II. s/o Elias Buell & Virda Ellen (Lucas) Garlinghouse. m. Florence (Schultz) 7 Nov 1942, children Linda, William "Bill," Terry and Jon.

GEORGIA - b. Jul 1894, Peru, Kan; d/o Arza H. & Sarah "Sadie" Elaine (Holmes) Garlinghouse. m. ... Simpson 1914, Clarkston, Wash., one child Richard.

GEORGIA ANN (Johnson) - b. 23 Dec 1937, CA; d. 17 Aug 1985, Los Angeles, CA; m. G. K. Garlinghouse.

GEORGIA MAY - b. 9 Nov 1895, Hillsdale, Vermillion Co., IN; d. 18 Jun 1972, Hillsdale, IN; Buried in Helt's Prairie Cem., Hillsdale, Vermillion Co., IN. d/o Sylvester R. & Lizzie White (Casebeer) Garlinghouse. m. Roy O. Boren 1 May 1913, children Wilma and Clara Mae. m2nd. (...) Kibby.

GEORGIANNA - b. 30 Jan 1863; d. 10 Sep 1899; d/o David B. & Mary A. (Davis) Garlinghouse.

GERALD - s/o Larry Garlinghouse.

GERALD ARZA - b. 1880, Neb; s/o Arza H. & Sarah "Sadie" Elaine (Holmes) Garlinghouse. m. Elizabeth (Gilbert) 1904, Kan, children Gerald Gilbert, Audrey, Rena, Marjie, Morse Nolan and Donald.

GERALD GILBERT - b. 1905, Lewiston, Idaho; s/o Gerald Arza & Elizabeth (Gilbert) Garlinghouse. One child Larry.

GERALD LLOYD - b. 6 Mar 1960, MI; s/o Robert Vernon & Lorna May (Wagner) Garlinghouse.

GERTRUDE (Harrison) - b. 1865, Minn; d. 20 Sep 1888, Aitkin Co., Minn; m. Ulysses Grant Garlinghouse, Aitkin, Minn.

GERTRUDE (Verheyen) - b. 1897, MO m. Fred Lee Garlinghouse 10 Oct 1919 or 9 Jun 1920, one child Robert Lee.

GERTRUDE (...) - m. ... Richardi. m2nd. Burton A. Garlinghouse 25 Jul 1942, CA.

GLADYS GRACE (Taylor) - b. 9 Jan 1911, St. John, Wash; d. Nov 1983, Boise, Idaho; m.

Lester Edwin Garlinghouse 8 Feb 1936, Salem, Oregon, Children Lawrence Edwin and Ellen Jane.

GLENWOOD K. - b. Feb 1887, OH; d. 1930, Johnstown, OH; s/o George E. & Caroline "Callie" S. (Knorr). m. Fern E. (...). m2nd. Hazel O. (Kendrick) 3 Oct 1925, Sunbury, Delaware Co., Ohio.

GORDON SPAULDING - b. 17 Sep 1910, Redmond, Oregon; d. 10 Oct 1910, Redmond, Oregon; s/o Lyman Edwin & Ida May (Spaulding) Garlinghouse.

GRACE (...) - m. Mervyn W. "Bud" Garlinghouse, children Donald L. and Carol.

GRACE (Mitchell) - d. about 1848, Wapello Co., Iowa; m. David Woodruff Garlinghouse 31 Jan 1839, White Co., IN, children Lovina "Savina" and Mary Jane.

GRACE (Shoemaker) - d. 1927-28; m. Monroe Garlinghouse children William "Bill," Roy, Ruth and Delmar.

GRACE JUNE - b. 1878, Naples, New York; d/o Samuel R. & Emily S. (Baker) Garlinghouse. m. Henry Louis Webster 15 Aug 1899, Rochester, New York, children Harold, Dorothy and Albert.

GRACIE - b. 8 Dec 1889, Newark, Essex Co., NJ; d. 5 Jun 1895; Buried in Fairmount Cemetery, Newark, NJ. d/o Joseph & Cora Bell (Johnson) Garlinghouse.

GRANT - b. 19 Nov 1866, Wayne, Steuben Co., New York; d. 12 Oct 1886, Bath, New York; s/o Daniel Benjamin & Sarah "Sally" (Margeson) Garlinghouse.

GRANT - Living at Acworth, GA in 1996.

GRANT WESLEY - b. 1928, Mekawele, Kauai, Hawaii; s/o Ralph Leman & Elizabeth Hayes (Davison) Garlinghouse. m. Barbara Irene (Frame) 1956, Newton, Iowa, children Wanda Leilana and Keith David.

GRETTA - m. Dean George Garlinghouse one child Margarett. Living at Sault Ste Marie, MI in 1996.

GRETCHEN ANN - b. 3 Jan 1947; d/o Richard Earl, M.D. & Miriam Esther (Thoroman) Garlinghouse. m. Dennis Gregg Huddleston 12 May 1974, one child Zachary Clark.

GURDON BENEDICT - b. 23 Nov 1854, Tecumseh, Mich; d. 15 Sep 1939, Tecumseh, Mich; s/o John Benedict & Mary Jane (Benedict) Garlinghouse. m. Minnie Minerva (Gates) 1879, children Clarissa Maye, Ethalyn Virginia, Otto Gates, Arnet John and his twin who died. m2nd. Mrs. Francis M. Bryan 1914, Tecumseh, Lenawee Co., Mich.

HALLIE J. - b. 1897, IN; d/o Edmund Oscar & Sarah (Wilson) Garlinghouse.

HANNAH - b. 30 Dec 1797, Ontario Co., New York; d. 17 Mar 1842, Leesville, Hart Co., KY; d/o James & Elanor "Eleanor" (Hunt) Garlinghouse. m. Silas Lee 9 Nov 1819, Elizabethtown, Hardin Co., KY, children Silas J.J., L.J., Samuel Lindsey, and H.L.

HANNAH "MA" - b. 15 Jan 1820, Vernon, NJ; d. 4 Jul 1906, Scotch Plains, NJ; d/o Gamaliel & Mary (Monroe) Garlinghouse. m. John Radley Marsh 6 Jul 1845, Newark, NJ, children Josephine, Mary Emma, John, George Wallace and Frank.

HANNAH - b. 1826, Hart Co., KY; d/o George & Elcy Lee (Drury) Garlinghouse. m. Crispin S. Bomar B/4 1850, KY, one child Thomas E.

HANNAH (McCarty) - b. Dec 1842, Ohio; m. James H. Garlinghouse, 3 Nov 1870, Wapello Co., Iowa, children William H., John E. and Mary L.

HAROLD - s/o ... Garlinghouse. Living at Colonia, NJ in 1996.

HAROLD - b.31 Jul 1942; d. Mar 1986; s/o ... Garlinghouse

HAROLD CHARLES - b. 5 Apr 1895; d. Mar 1973, Denver, Colo; s/o Almond Jewett & Laura Elma (Hayden) Garlinghouse, one child Donald Albert.

HAROLD JAMES - b. 6 Feb 1917, New York; d. 17 Nov 1974, Ellenville, New York; He served as seaman 2nd Class in US Navy during WW II; s/o Ira David & Esther Anna (Reed) Garlinghouse. m. Catherine M. (Spence), children Patricia E., Harold James, Jr. and Edward Joseph. m2nd. Doris (...) 1960.

HAROLD JAMES, JR. - b. 9 May 1941, Ellenville, New York; d. 7 Aug 1966, he was killed in an auto accident at Spring Glen, New York; He is buried at Fantinekill Cem., Ellenville, New York. s/o Harold James & Catherine M. (Spence) Garlinghouse. m. Beverly (Worlock).

HARRIET - b. 1856, Vlg. Twp., Van Buren Co., Iowa; d/o Thomas Briggs & Augusta (Demmett) Garlinghouse.

HARRIET (White) - b. @ 1870; m. Franklin Garlinghouse.

HARRY W. - s/o ... Garlinghouse. Living at Oakville, WA in 1996.

HATTIE (Cory) - b. 11 May 1859; d. 10 Dec 1949; m. Isaac Ashton Garlinghouse 10 Nov 1880, Barrington, New York, children Leo C., Ruby Nellie and Pearl.

HATTIE "NETTA" - b. 1868, IN; d/o George Perry & Sarah "Sally" E. (Cotton) Garlinghouse. m. Willis "Wellby" Monroe 15 Jul 1887.

HATTIE - b. 1878, Kan; d. B/4 13 Apr 1898; d/o Martin V. & Sarah Ann (Long) Garlinghouse.

HATTIE B. (Nolan) - b. IL; d. at age 55, FL; m. James Garlinghouse 30 Sep 1890, Hendricks Co., IN, one child John Ulmont. m2nd. W. A. Sanges.

HAZEL "HASEL" "HEC" RUPERT - b. 22 Dec 1889, Denver, Colo; d. Dec 1963, Wash; s/o Arza H. & Sarah "Sadie" Elaine (Holmes) Garlinghouse.

m. Lucy A. (...).

HAZEL O. (Kendrick) - b. 9 Sep 1894, Mt. Sterling, Ohio; m. ... Williams. m2nd. Glenwood K. Garlinghouse 3 Oct 1925, Sunbury, Delaware Co., Ohio. m3rd. Archie E. Lowry.

HEGGIE - d/o George B. & Josie (Robison) Garlinghouse.

HELEN - b. 1902, Clinton, NY; d/o John Newton & Julia Allerton (Stebbins) Garlinghouse. m. Harold King.

HELEN (Bulkley) - b. 26 May 1905, Mich; d. Jun 1974, Grosse Pointe Woods, Mich; m. John G. Garlinghouse 12 Oct 1935, one child Susan.

HELEN D. - b. 13 Jul 1898; d/o Franklin Bennett & Lilly M. (Grady) Garlinghouse. m. Mart Hamilton 14 Apr 1915, Spencer Co., IN. m2nd. John G. Dertz.

HELEN M. - b. about 1909, CA; d/o Orville & Violet (...) Garlinghouse.

HELEN MATILDA (Vossbrinck) - b. 3 Mar 1911, Brooklyn, Kings Co., New York; m. Nelson Asa Garlinghouse 9 Oct 1948, one son Kent Nelson.

HELLEN (Israel) - m. John G. Garlinghouse 27 Jul 1862, Vevay, Switzerland Co., IN.

HELLIN "HELLEN" (Salisbury) - b. 1845, IL; m. George C. Garlinghouse 20 Jul 1863, McDonough Co., IL, children Evelyn "Evia", Fred W., Opal, Clyde S. and Mavis.

HENRY - b. 1844, IN; s/o Josiah & Amanda (Belknap) Garlinghouse. m. Eliza (...), children Ellen J., Mary M., Lucy, James R. and Ida Myrtle.

HENRY - b. @ 1850; s/o (...) Gardenhouse (sic).

He had a son, b. 11 Oct 1875, Newark, NJ.

HENRY - b. 1863, Iowa; s/o Lacy & Elizabeth (McCormick) Garlinghouse. m. Eliza (...), children Lacy and Ida.

HENRY - b. 1866, Colo; s/o Andrew Leonard & America J. (Bradburn) Garlinghouse.

HENRY ELMER NATHAN - b. 1 Oct 1907, Madison, Jefferson Co., IN; s/o Ulysses Arthur & Mary Erskine (Davis) Garlinghouse.

HERBERT - b. 1 Nov 1912, Hillsdale, Vermillion Co., IN; d. Aug 1979, Peru, IN; s/o Hugh A. & Eva O. (Watson) Garlinghouse. m. Frances (DeVerter). He served in U.S. Army in W.W.2.

HERBERT HOOVER - s/o David Bryan & Ethel (Card) Garlinghouse. m. Mary Lou (...), one child Mark.

HILDA - b. 1910, Ohio; d/o Reid & Sue E. "Lou" (Miller) Garlinghouse.

HILDA (Goetz) - m. ... Moini. m2nd. David Bryan Garlinghouse, Jr. 12 May 1973

HIRAM - b. 19 Aug 1853, Delaware Co., Ohio; d. 24 Feb 1858, Van Buren Co., Iowa; Buried in White Chapel Cem., Lick Creek Twp., Van Buren Co., Iowa. s/o Silas & Margaret (Reid) Garlinghouse.

HOLMES SPALDING - b. Jan 1860, Canandaigua, New York; d. 1942, Glendale, CA; s/o Leman B. & Martha Ann (Spalding) Garlinghouse. m. Emma Permelia (Sherman) 16 Dec 1885, Leadville, Colo., children Sherman, Leslie Holmes, Ralph Leman and Albert Frederick.

HOMER - s/o ... Garlinghouse. m. Lee (...). Living at Lebanon, OR in 1996.

HOSITA "HARRIETT" - b. 1826, New York; d/o

Stephen A. & Elizabeth "Betsy" (Roberts) Garlinghouse.

HOWARD N. - b. 1892, Ohio; d. 1910, Ohio; s/o William E. & Luella (Crego) Garlinghouse.

HUGH A. - b. 26 Mar 1888, Hillsdale, Vermillion Co., IN; d. 30 Nov 1920, Hillsdale, IN; He is buried in Helt's Prairie Cem., Vermillion Co., IN. s/o Sylvester R. & Lizzie White (Casebeer) Garlinghouse. m. Eva O. (Watson), children Herbert, Mangnia Elizabeth and Treva.

I.R. (...) - m. ... Garlinghouse. Living at Seattle, WA in 1996.

IDA "JAMES J." (...) - b. June 1854, New York; m. Arthur B. Garlinghouse, one child J. Merle

IDA - b. 1 Jul 1859, Newark, NJ; d. 13 Jan 1866, Newark, NJ; d/o John & Sarah (Polhemus) Garlinghouse.

IDA (Tomkins) - b. 1872, PA; m. Frederick L. Garlinghouse 1891, one child Richard.

IDA - b. 1874, Minn; d/o Lacy & Elizabeth (McCormick) Garlinghouse. m. Henry Comstock, children Verndella, Emma, Addie and Henry, Jr.

IDA - b. @ 1888; d/o Henry & Eliza (...) Garlinghouse.

IDA B. - d/o Joseph & Cora Bell (Johnson) Garlinghouse. m. Cortland P. Fortenbach 1920, children H. and L. B.

IDA BELLE - d/o John & Emma (Card) Garlinghouse.

IDA E. - b. 31 Mar 1869, Ann Arbor, Mich; d/o Nelson S. & Mary E. (Willitts) Garlinghouse. m. Arthur Jones 15 May 1901.

IDA ELENA - b. 31 Oct 1896, Madison, Jefferson Co., NJ; d. 22 Dec 1970; d/o Willard Elmer & Mary Elizabeth (Ashley) Garlinghouse. m. Earl Lupton, children Janice Lefern, Anita Rose, Earl Kieth and Don Allen.

IDA MAY (Spaulding) - b. 15 Nov 1873, Faribault, Minn; d. 3 Mar 1960, Halfway, OR. m. ... Sager. m2nd. Lyman Edwin Garlinghouse 1 Apr 1908, Portland, OR, children Margaret, Gordon Spaulding, Lester Edwin and Ace Nelson.

IDA MYRTLE - b. Mar 1880, Minn; d/o Henry & Eliza (...) Garlinghouse.

IKE - s/o Ira W. Garlinghouse.

ILEEN - b. 1920, CA; d/o Orville & Violet (...) Garlinghouse.

IMOGENE (Shaw) - m. ... Ferguson. m2nd. Benjamin Porter Garlinghouse 1938.

IMOGENE (Boggs) - b. 19 Oct 1911; d. Oct 1986, Dallas, TX; m. Wendell Lewis Garlinghouse.

INA BELL - b. 4 Oct 1871, KS; d. Aug 1872, KS; d/o Lucian Bonaparte & Matilda Ruth (Hanawalt) Garlinghouse.

INEZ FLORENCE - b. 16 Aug 1919; d/o George Howard & Margaret (Stephenson) Garlinghouse. m. Dale Short, children Ronald Dale and Janice Gail.

IRA BURCHFIELD - b. 18 Dec 1896, MI; d. 23 May 1982, Bay City, MI; s/o John Edward & Effie Gertrude (Perrine) Garlinghouse. m. Iva Mable (Abeare) 1923, MI, children Lovilla Gertrude, Loren Ira, Joyce Iva & Beverly Ann.

IRA DAVID - b. 10 Aug 1891, Hancock, Del. Co., New York; d. 17 Feb 1980, Ellenville, New York; s/o James & Anna (Bennet) Garlinghouse. m. Esther Anna (Reed), children Esther, Harold James, Charles R. and Ira W.

IRA G. - s/o ... Garlinghouse. m. F. (...). Living at Delray Beach, FL in 1996.

IRA REED - b. 25 Jan 1833, New York; d. 30 Aug 1910, Mich; s/o David & Margaret Jane (Coryell) Garlinghouse. m. Melissa A. (Coryell) 1856, children Adelbert E., John Edward, Etha and Anna May.

IRA W - s/o Ira David & Esther (Reed) Garlinghouse. He married twice. 1st marriage children Nancy and Ike. m2nd Judy (Furman), children boy-girl twins and boy.

IRENA JANE "June" - b. @ 1825, IN; d/o John & Louanna (Bennett) Garlinghouse. m. Alexander McCormick 25 Jan 1844, White Co., IN, children Thomas, Elizabeth, William, James A. and Loanna.

IRENE - d/o Levi Curtis & Eva (Stuart) Garlinghouse. m. Hyman Greenstein, one child Curtis.

IRENE (Laird) - b. 5 Jun 1920, Dayton, Ohio; m. George Willard "Billy" Garlinghouse 5 Feb 1946, Madison, IN.

IRENE (Reynolds) - m. Valnor C. Garlinghouse.

IRENE MAY - b. 1918; d/o Sherman & Ella (...) Garlinghouse.

IRMA (...) - m. Burton A. Garlinghouse.

ISAAC - b. 16 Dec 1833, Hart Co., KY; d. 24 Oct 1850, Hart Co., KY; s/o George & Elcy Lee (Drury) Garlinghouse.

ISAAC ASHTON, M.D. - b. 9 Oct 1852, Wayne, Steuben Co., New York; d. 30 Nov 1916, prob. Kan; He was medical examiner for sub-district of Kansas City, MO. s/o Daniel Benjamin & Mary (Margeson) Garlinghouse. m. Hattie (Cory) 10 Nov 1880, Barrington, New York, children Leo C., Ruby Nellie and Pearl.

ISABEL A. - b. Sep 1870, Oregon; d. 24 Jan 1937, Orange Co., CA; d/o Stephen & Prudence W. (Howard) Sanders Garlinghouse.

ISABELLA JOLLY (DeWitt) - b. 13 Feb 1822, PA; d. 23 Mar 1863, Switzerland Co., IN; m. George Bennett Garlinghouse, children George Perry, Aurelius DeWitt, Paulina Jane, John Francis Oscar, Levi Curtis, Charles Oliver, Viola Mariah and Francesco Bruce.

IVA MABLE (Abeare) - b. 1904; m. Ira Birchfield Garlinghouse 1923, children Lovilla Gertrude, Loren Ira, Joyce Iva and Beverly Ann.

J. (...) - m. ... Garlinghouse. Living at Paradise, CA in 1996.

J. B. - Living at Reno, Nevada in 1996.

J. E. - Living at Lakeland, FL in 1996.

J. MERLE - b. Jan 1882, Kan; d. young, Kan; s/o Arthur B. & Ida "James J." (...) Garlinghouse.

J. WOODROW - s/o Elias B. & Virda Ellen (Lucas) Garlinghouse.

JAC - b. 1934, Lewiston, Idaho; s/o Richard Lynn Garlinghouse. Children Staci Dawn and Jill.

JAMES - Baptized 1773, Old School Baptist Church, Warwick, New York; d. 1790, Vernon, Sussex Co., NJ; He was wounded during an Indian raid at Ft. Hamilton, Stroudsburg, PA, 11 Dec 1757. He also served in the Revolutionary War. Prob. s/o John George Garlinghouse. m. Joanna (Buchanan), children Abigail, John, Joseph, Benjamin, James, Marcia, Stephen, Thomas and Gamaliel.

JAMES - b. Jan or Feb 1765, NJ; d. 2 Oct 1850, Delaware Co., Ohio; Prob. s/o James & Joanna (Buchanan) Garlinghouse. m. Elanor "Eleanor" (Hunt), children Catherine, Mary Ann "Polly", twins Jane & Gamaliel, Hannah, George, Rachel, Silas, Martha "Patty" and Eleanor.

JAMES - b. 25 Apr 1809, Vernon, Sussex Co., NJ; d. 26 Aug 1832; Vernon, Sussex Co., NJ; s/o Gamaliel & Mary (Monroe) Garlinghouse.

JAMES - b. 1854, New York; s/o David B. & Mary

A. (Davis). m. Anna (Bennet), children Willard, Ira David, Mary "May" and Eva.

JAMES - b. 1870, Hillsdale, Vermillion Co., IN; d. 1895; s/o Cyrenus A. & Sarah A. (Jackson) Garlinghouse. m. Hattie B. (Nolan) 30 Sep 1890, Hendricks Co., IN, one child John Ulmont.

JAMES AMSEY - b. 21 Sep 1915, Sussex Co., NJ; d. 5 Feb 1971; s/o John & Emma (Card) Garlinghouse.

JAMES ARMSTRONG - b. 1964, Pasadena, CA; s/o Albert Frederick & Barbara Evlyn (Myers) Garlinghouse.

JAMES BUELL "Bub" - b. 28 Feb 1907, Lebanon, Colo; d. 6 Feb 1990, Lewis, Montezuma Co., Colo. s/o Elias Buell & Virda Ellen (Lucas) Garlinghouse. m. Ruth Huckabay 16 Mar 1935, Cortez, Colo., children Edward Buell, James and Carolyn.

JAMES H. - b. 1828, Hart Co., KY; d. 1877-80, Wapello Co., Iowa; s/o George & Elcy Lee (Drury) Garlinghouse. m. Hannah (McCarty) 3 Nov 1870, Eddyville, Wapello Co., Iowa, children William H., John E. and Mary L.

JAMES L. - b. 27 Jan 1786; d. 15 May 1836, Plains Twp., Franklin Co., Ohio; He served in the War of 1812 as a private under Captain Nathaniel Fisher and Colonel Philitus Swift in the 2nd Regiment of New York Militia from Sep 1812 to Dec 1813. s/o John & Jane (Leonard) Garlinghouse. m. Susannah (Belknap), children Arthur, Josiah, Benjamin, Jesse, Sarah, Juliette and Ann Eliza(Beth).

JAMES MANUS - b. 13 Sep 1981, Topeka, Shawnee Co., Kan; s/o Whitney Beard & Nancy Ruth (Manus) Garlinghouse.

JAMES MITCHELL - b. 1864, Licking Co., Ohio;

s/o Josiah & Amanda (Belknap) Garlinghouse. m. Mary Elizabeth (Seaton) 8 Aug 1863, Mille Lacs, Minn.

JAMES R. - b. 1874, Minn; s/o Henry & Eliza (...) Garlinghouse.

JAMES RUFUS - b. 17 Jul 1901, Aitkin Co., Minn; d. Jan 1985, Elma, Wash; s/o William Josiah & Elizabeth Howe (Campbell) Garlinghouse. m. Marie (...). m2nd. Bertha E. (...) Price 7 Feb 1970, Tacoma, Wash.

JAMES RUSSELL - b. 3 Nov 1948, Lewis, Montezuma Co., Colo; s/o James Buell & Ruth (Huckaby) Garlinghouse. m. Kay (Rorck), children Marc and Monica.

JANE (Leonard) - b. 25 Jul 1763; d. 27 May 1841, Hemlock, New York; Buried in St. Paul's Churchyard, Allen's Hill, Ontario Co., New York. m. John Garlinghouse, children Joseph, James L., John G., Joanna, Benjamin, Elizabeth "Betsy", Sally, Mary and Leonard. m2nd. Moses Briggs about 1811, Richmond, New York.

JANE - b. 26 Mar 1792, Luzerne Co., PA; Twin of Gamaliel. d. 10 Dec 1876, Benton Co., Oregon; Buried in Alpine Cem., Benton Co., Oregon. d/o James & Elanor "Eleanor" (Hunt) Garlinghouse. m. Jesse Belknap 20 Feb 1812, Ontario Co., New York, children Kesia, Hannah, George, Ransom Amos, Talitha Cumi, Corrington Gavitt and Harley Augustus.

JANE - b. 8 Dec 1809, Ontario Co., New York; d. 3 Oct 1851, West Avon, New York; d/o Joseph & Submit (Sheldon) Garlinghouse. m. Orville Comstock, children Delphine, Isabel "Belle", Samuel, Alice M., Pinckney and Jane.

JANE - b. 8 Aug 1814, Sussex Co., NJ; d. 16 Apr 1901, Bath, Steuben Co., New York; d/o Thomas & Polly "Mary" (Benjamin) Garlinghouse. m.

Gurdon Lathrop Webster 12 Jan 1841, Urbana, Steuben Co., New York, children Lester Garlinghouse, Byron Almond and John Gurdon.

JANE (Russell) - b. 11 May 1948, Port Jefferson, NY; d. 29 Jul 1973, Ellenville, New York; Buried in Fantinekill Cem., Ellenville, NY. m. Edward Joseph Garlinghouse 21 Oct 1967, Ellenville, NY, children Diane Russell, William and Edward.

JANE "JENNIE" DELPHINE - b. 25 Feb 1846, Allen's Hill, Ontario Co., New York; d. 15 Mar 1928, Mt. Morris, New York; Buried in Mt. Morris Cem., Mt, Morris, New York. d/o John Nelson & Lorinda (Short) Garlinghouse. m. Frederick P. Mills Feb 1872, children Frederick Peter, Jr. and a child deceased. m2nd. George M. Shull 12 Mar 1891, Mt. Morris, New York.

JANE ESTHER - b. 26 Jun 1943; d/o Robert Orestes, M.D. & Esther Winifred (Coghill) Garlinghouse. m. Melvin N. Beal 1 Jan 1964, children Rebecca Jane and Amy Clark.

JANET - b. 17 Apr 1948; d/o Arnet John & Jean (Stewart) Garlinghouse. m. Kerry Lawrence.

JANET ELIZABETH - b. 5 Jan 1952, Elgin, IL; d/o Charles A. & Wilhelmine "Wilma" E. (Menzen) Garlinghouse. m. Dennis E. Tiberius, Jr. 14 May 1971, Los Angeles, CA, children Charles Edward, Anna Elizabeth and Leah Emilie. m2nd. Mark Edwards 26 Apr 1986, Cocoa Beach, FL. m3rd. Richard Donaho 1 Jan 1988, Cozumel, Mexico.

JANET MARILYN (Morse) - b. 1948, Prosser, Wash; m. John Jay Garlinghouse 1974.

JASON - b. Sep 1974; d. Sep 1974; s/o Kent Nelson & Rosemary (Gutierrez) Garlinghouse.

JASPER SYLVESTER - b. 25 Feb 1850, Wapello Co.,

Iowa; d. 15 Sep 1903, Aitkin, Minn; s/o David Woodruff & Catherine (Garlinghouse) Garlinghouse. m. Rhoda Harriet (DuPey) 30 Oct 1876, Aitkin, Minn, children Cynthia, Dolly, Edward Sylvester and a female infant, who died at three months.

JEAN (...) - m. Robert Lee Garlinghouse one child Beth. Living at Rome, NY in 1996.

JEAN (Stewart) - b. 1920; m. Arnet John Garlinghouse 1944, children Susan, Janet and Kathleen.

JEAN (...) - m. ... Garlinghouse. Living at Benton, TN in 1996.

JEANNE (...) - m. Jennings Woodrow "Woodie" Garlinghouse 28 Jun 1951, adopted children Rodney and Katherine.

JEANNETTE M. (Pyme) - b. 26 Feb 1887, Gap Mills, W. VA; m. ... Leslie. m2nd. Earl Leo Garlinghouse 12 Oct 1926, Delaware Co., Ohio.

JEANNETTE MADGE - b. 4 Jan 1924; d/o Edward Sylvester & Emma (Shae) Garlinghouse. m. Oliver Olson.

JEFFREY - Living at West Henrietta, NY in 1996.

JEFFREY LOUIS - b. 9 Apr 1966, Sault Ste. Marie, MI; s/o Jerry Louis & Ruby Mary (Long) Garlinghouse.

JENNIE C. - b. 11 Sep 1885, Sussex Co., NJ; d. 1974; d/o John Monroe & Jesteen D. (Farber) Garlinghouse. m. Arthur Widner, children John, Raymond and Myrtle.

JENNIE MAY - b. 19 Sep 1864, Worthington, Iowa; d. 26 Apr 1907, Worthington, Iowa; d/o Darius Hill & Minerva Jane "Jennie" (White)

Garlinghouse. m. Isaac Evan Littlefield 17 May 1882, children Arthur Evan and Jennie Olive. m2nd. Frederick Ratcliff 23 Aug 1888, children Frederick Darius, Ida May, John Edwin, Nelson Frank, Orpha Grace, Manley Lawton, Jessie Mary Ann and Minerva Susanna.

JENNIFER LYNN - b. 23 Mar 1976, San Diego, CA; d/o Lester David & Diane Lynn (Bernard) Garlinghouse.

JENNINGS BRYAN "Biggin" "Tex" - b. 30 Mar 1915, Lebanon, Montezuma Co., Colo; He served as Master Sergeant in the US Army in the South Pacific during World War II; s/o Elias Buell & Virda Ellen (Lucas) Garlinghouse. m. Patricia (Rowberry) 17 Oct 1946, one child Toni Ann.

JENNINGS WOODROW "WOODIE" - b. 30 Jun 1913, Lebanon, Montezuma Co., Colo; s/o Elias Buell & Virda Ellen (Lucas) Garlinghouse. m. Jeanne (...) 28 Jun 1951, adopted children Rodney and Katherine.

JEREMIAH "GERALD" - b. Oct 1855, Iowa; s/o Benjamin & Catherine Maria (Williams) Garlinghouse. m. (...), one child Ethel. m2nd. Bessie (...) before 1900 Census, children Lynn and Treva.

JERRY LOUIS - b. 8 May 1936, Sault Ste. Marie, MI; s/o Mark & Elizabeth Victoria (Pope) Garlinghouse. m. Ruby Mary (Long) 20 Jun 1959, Sault Ste. Marie, MI, children Donna Ruby, Connie Jean, Karen Lynn, Jeffrey Louis and Joseph Mark.

JERRY W - s/o William L. Garlinghouse. Living at Globe, AZ in 1996.

JESSE - b. 1815-20; s/o James L. & Susannah (Belknap) Garlinghouse.

JESSIE E. "BESSIE" - b. Oct 1872, Hillsdale,

Vermillion Co., IN; d/o Cyrenus A. & Sarah A. (Jackson) Garlinghouse. m. Charles E. Selch 19 Jun 1889, Vermillion Co., IN, one child Hershell. m2nd. (...) Douglas.

JESSE MABEL - b. 12 Jul 1882, Worthington, Iowa; d. 19 Oct 1952, Perth, ND; d/o Darius Hill & Minerva Jane "Jennie" (White) Garlinghouse. m. William Gelvin 14 Aug 1901, children Florence Evelyn, Mabel Elizabeth, Grover G., Melvin L., John W. and Myrtle E. m2nd. Carl Berg 2 Jun 1925.

JESTEEN D. (Farber) - b. 29 Mar 1859, New York; d. 29 Jul 1920, Vernon, Sussex Co., NJ; m. John Monroe Garlinghouse 25 Apr 1880, children Sherwood Benjamin, Katherine Elizabeth, Jennie C., John, Monroe, Vernon and Frank Dewey.

JILL - b. about 1966, Lewiston, Idaho; d/o Jac Garlinghouse.

JOANN B. (Nicol) - b. 2 Jan 1941; d. 23 Aug 1969; m. Donald L. Garlinghouse 11 Jan 1957, children Tammi, Terri and Timothy.

JOANNA (Buchanan) - Baptized 1773, Old School Baptist Church, Warwick, New York; Prob. m. James Garlinghouse, children Abigail, John, Joseph, Benjamin, James, Marcia, Stephen, Thomas and Gamaliel. She moved to Chemung Co., New York, 1795.

JOANNA - b. 30 Jun 1790; d. 31 Oct 1857, Ontario Co., New York; d/o John & Jane (Leonard) Garlinghouse. Buried in Purcell Rd. Cem., Ontario Co., New York.

JOANNA "ANN" - b. 10 Sep 1811, Sussex Co., NJ; d. 6 Feb 1894, Tecumseh, Lenawee Co., Mich; d/o Thomas & Polly "Mary" (Benjamin) Garlinghouse. m. John Finch, children Julia and Ornan B.

JOHN - b. 10 Oct 1758; d. 12 Aug 1810, Hemlock, Ontario Co., New York; Buried in St. Paul's Churchyard, Allen's Hill, Ontario Co., New York. He served in the Revolutionary War as Private in Captain Cyrus Beckwith's Company, 2nd Regiment. Also the Continental Army and the New York Levies in Captain Goodwin's Company in Colonel Frederick Weissenfeld's Regiment. He was also in DuBoy's Regiment of New York Levies. Probably s/o James & Joanna (Buchanan) Garlinghouse. m. Jane (Leonard), children Joseph, James L., John G., Joanna, Benjamin, Elizabeth "Betsy", Sally, Mary and Leonard.

JOHN - b. 1 Nov 1811, Vernon, Sussex Co., NJ; d. 21 Nov 1887, Warwick, New York; s/o Gamaliel & Mary (Monroe) Garlinghouse. m. Catherine Elizabeth (Utter) 2 Jan 1843, children Silas, John Monroe, Colina, Caroline Mary, Cathren J. and a daughter.

JOHN - b. 8 Jul 1831, NJ; d. 5 Apr 1863, Newark, NJ; s/o Joseph & Maria (Ryerson) Garlinghouse. m. Sarah (Polhemus) 24 Feb 1856, Newark, NJ, children George, Joseph, Ida and John.

JOHN - b. 18 Nov 1862, Newark, NJ; d. 28 Feb 1863, Newark, NJ; s/o John & Sarah (Polhemus) Garlinghouse.

JOHN - b. 20 Nov 1887, Sussex Co., NJ; d. 9 Feb 1963, Sussex Co., NJ; s/o John Monroe & Jesteen D. (Farber) Garlinghouse. m. Emma (Card), children James Amsey and Ida Belle.

JOHN - bap. 31 Jul 1950, Bergen Co., NJ; s/o ... Garlinghouse. m. Anna M. (Robertson).

JOHN - Living at Indianoplis, IN in 1996.

JOHN - s/o Arnet John, III. Living at Lansing, MI in 1996.

JOHN ANDREW - b. 1848, Hart Co., KY; s/o George & Elcy Lee (Drury) Garlinghouse. m. Laura M. (Vancleave) 27 Oct, 1878, Wapello Co., Iowa, children Elsa G., a son, a dau. and George M.

JOHN BENEDICT - b. 17 Feb 1825, New York; d. 1 Dec 1892, Tecumseh, Lenawee Co., MI s/o Thomas & Polly "Mary" (Benjamin) Garlinghouse. m. Mary Jane (Benedict) 10 Dec 1850, Warwick, Orange Co., New York, children Gurdon Benedict, twins Burton A. and Benson J.

JOHN CORYELL - b. 9 Aug 1838, Macon, Mich; d. 30 Jan 1924, Napoleon, Mich; He served during the Civil War for one year beginning 15 Dec 1864. s/o David & Margaret Jane (Coryell) Garlinghouse. m. Alice C. (Vining) Seaman 23 Dec 1896, Jackson Co., Mich.

JOHN DANIEL - b. 21 Mar 1936, Madison, IN; d. 5 Apr 1974, Madison, IN; s/o George Howard & Mildred (Jones) Garlinghouse.

JOHN E. - b. Nov 1875, Wapello Co., Iowa; s/o James H. Garlinghouse.

JOHN E. - Living at Kileen, TX in 1996.

JOHN EDWARD - b. 1866, MI; d. 1930; s/o Ira Reed & Melissa A. (Coryell) Garlinghouse. m. Effie Gertrude (Perrine) 20 Nov 1895, children Ira Burchfield, John Raymond, Elton Ellsworth and Vernon Lloyd. m2nd. Carrie (...) between 1915 and 1920.

JOHN EDWARD - b. 8 Jun 1991, Lawrenceville, GA. s/o Walter Sheldon, III & Donna Marie (Schwieter) Garlinghouse.

JOHN ELSWORTH - b. 1952; s/o Junior Ellsworth & Lucy (Gascho) Garlinghouse. m. Cathy (...).

JOHN FRANCIS OSCAR - b. 1 Dec 1849, IN; s/o George Bennett & Isabella Jolly (DeWitt) Garlinghouse. m. Josephine "Rose" O. (McFadden) 27 Aug 1870, Jefferson Co., IN, one child Charles "Charley" W. m2nd. Mary E. (McClure) 15 Jan 1879, Madison, Jefferson Co., IN, children Bess, Mabel and Fred Bartlett.

JOHN G. - b. 20 Jun 1788, Schuylkill, PA; d. @ 1860, Effingham Co., IL; He served in the War of 1812. His grave is marked with a Government headstone that states "US Soldier War of 1812;" Buried in Freemanton Cem., Effingham Co., IL. s/o John & Jane (Leonard) Garlinghouse. m. Lewanna "Louanna" (Bennett), children David Woodruff, Cyrus Buell, Submit S., Benjamin, George Bennett, Thomas Briggs, Lucy Irene and Andrew Leonard.

JOHN G. - b. 1838, prob. White Co., IN; s/o Cyrus Buell & Cassiah "Keziah" (Nichols) Garlinghouse. m. Hellen (Israel) 27 Jul 1862, Switzerland Co., IN.

JOHN G. - b. 7 Apr 1903, Mich; d. Jun 1988; Grosse Pointe Woods, MI. s/o Benson J. & Margaret C. "Mary" (Gray) Garlinghouse. m. Helen (Bulkley) 12 Oct 1935. One child Susan.

JOHN GEORGE - A petition to the Court of Quarter Sessions, Bucks Co., PA, 1748 (to create Smithfield Twp.), had John Garlinghouse as a signator. On 18 Feb 1750, John George Gernhousen (sic) obtained a warrant for 50 acres in Smithfield Twp. He had one child, James.

JOHN J. - b. 23 Apr 1903, Vernon, Sussex Co., NJ; d. Feb 1974, Clearwater, FL; s/o Sherwood Benjamin & Elizabeth (DeGraw) Garlinghouse.

JOHN MONROE - b. 29 Aug 1849, Sussex Co., NJ; d. 1925, Sussex Co., NJ; s/o John & Catherine

Elizabeth (Utter) Garlinghouse. m. Jesteen D. (Farber) 25 Apr 1880, children Sherwood Benjamin, Katherine Elizabeth, Jennie C., John, Monroe, Vernon and Frank Dewey.

JOHN NELSON - b. 14 Dec 1812, Allen's Hill, Ontario Co., New York; d. 27 Apr 1895, Allen's Hill, New York; Buried in St. Paul's Churchyard, Allen's Hill, Ontario Co., New York. s/o Joseph & Submit (Sheldon) Garlinghouse. m. Lorinda (Short) 24 May 1836, children Arabella "Belle" Louise and Jane "Jennie" Delphine. m2nd. Lucy West (Bothwell) 15 Oct 1853, children Abigail Mary, Joseph Milton, Nellie Bothwell, Emma L., Stoughton Tracy, Adelaide "Addie" L. and Fanny B.

JOHN NEWTON - b. 17 Mar 1876, Mt. Morris, New York; d. 18 May 1945, Clinton, New York; s/o Joseph & Chloe Rebecca (Beardsley) Garlinghouse, Jr. m. Julia Allerton (Stebbins) 5 Dec 1900, St. James Church, Clinton, New York, one child Helen. He was a dentist in Clinton, Oneida Co., NY.

JOHN NEWTON - b. 14 Jun 1935; s/o George L. & Dorothy (Rogers) Garlinghouse.

JOHN RAYMOND - b. 1901, Mich; d. 27 Dec 1980, Petoskey, MI; s/o John Edward & Effie Gertrude (Perrine) Garlinghouse. m. Genevieve May (Aldread) 1926, children Phyllis Marguerite, Ray Alden and Carol.

JOHN S. - s/o ... Garlinghouse. Living at Salt Lake City, UT in 1996.

JOHN SPALDING - b. Dec 1958, Madison, Wisc; s/o Ralph Spalding & Ellen (Ekman) Garlinghouse.

JOHN ULMONT - b. 6 Aug 1891, Hillsdale, Vermillion Co., IN; d. 23 Jan 1962, Capistrano Beach, CA; s/o James & Hattie B. (Nolan) Garlinghouse. m. Eva "Elizabeth" (...), one child Dorothy. m2nd. Mary Inez

(Hilliard).

JON - s/o George William & Florence (Schultz) Garlinghouse.

JON JAY - b. 1946, Spokane, Wash; s/o Morse Nolan & Dorothy Lillian (Roessell) Garlinghouse. m. Janet Marilyn (Morse) 1974.

JONATHAN - On 8 Jun 1746, the families in Hunter's Settlement, plus others on the North branch of the Delaware River petitioned to organize a Township. Jonathan Garlinghous (sic) was a signator.

JOSEPH - b. 1760; d. 28 Sep 1781; He served in the Revolutionary War as Private, Corporal and Sergeant during four enlistments. First as Private in Captain Beckwith's Company, 2nd Regiment of Sussex County, New Jersey Militia. Second as Private from 23 May 1778 to 14 Mar 1779 in Captain William Helm's Company, 2nd Regiment of New Jersey under the command of Colonel Israel Shreve. Third as Corporal from 1 May 1779 to 1 Jan 1780 in Captain Robert Wood's Company of New Levies in Lt. Colonel Albert Pawling's Regiment of New York Militia. Fourth as Corporal from 16 June 1781 to 28 Aug 1781 in Captain James Bonnell's Company of New Jersey Troops stationed on the frontiers in the County of Sussex. He was killed at Minisink on 28 Aug 1781, and was then shown as Sergeant. s/o James & Joanna (Buchanan) Garlinghouse.

JOSEPH - b. 14 Sep 1784, Sussex Co., NJ; d. 22 Feb 1862, LeRoy, Genesee Co., New York; Buried in St. Paul's Churchyard, Allen's Hill, Ontario Co., New York. He served during the War of 1812 from the last of December 1813 to 1 Apr 1814 in Captain Asa Wilder's Company in the Horse Regiment of New York State Militia. Also in Captain Asabel Warner's Company of Mounted Volunteers in Lt. Colonel Seymour Boughton's Regiment. He was present at the burning of Buffalo; He was elected sheriff of Ontario Co., New York for two terms, (1826-1828) & (1835-1837). He also served as Constable for 17 years. s/o John & Jane (Leonard) Garlinghouse. m. Submit (Sheldon) 12 Oct 1808, Williamstown, MA, children Jane, John Nelson, Leman Benton, Reuben S., William S., Laura, Joseph, Jr., Louise A., Mary, Ellen and Amelia S.

JOSEPH - b. 25 Dec 1791, NJ; d. 20 Nov 1836, Jacksonville, Morris Co., NJ; He served in the War of 1812 from September 1814 to 2 Dec 1814 in Captain Nathaniel Board's Company in Lt. Colonel Dodd's Regiment of New Jersey Militia. m. Maria "Mary" (Ryerson) 5 Jul 1811, Pompton, NJ, children Mary, Eliza, Ellen, Catherine, John and Louisa.

JOSEPH, Jr. - b. 21 Jun 1821, Richmond, Ontario Co., New York; d. 16 Jun 1876, Mt. Morris, New York. He served in the Civil War from 11 Aug 1864 to 2 Dec 1864 as 1st Lt., Quartermaster in the 58th Regiment of the 7th Division, of the 30th Brigade of New York National Guard; s/o Joseph & Submit (Sheldon) Garlinghouse. m. Rebecca (Stout) Hawley Poyntell. m2nd. Chloe Rebecca (Beardsley) 4 Feb 1869, St. James Church, Clinton, New York, children Anna Louise and John Newton.

JOSEPH - b. 14 Aug 1857, Newark, NJ; d. 6 Apr 1926, Newark, NJ; s/o John & Sarah (Polhemus) Garlinghouse. m. Cora Bell (Johnson) 22 Sep 1886, Newark, NJ, children Ida B. and Sarah C.

JOSEPH - b. Apr 1890, Kinross, Chippewa Co., MI; d. 1967; s/o Ulysses Grant Garlinghouse. m. Mary (Berkland), Chippewa Co., MI, they had one child who died young.

JOSEPH - s/o ... Garlinghouse. m. Kristen (...). Living at Ann Arbor, MI in 1996.

JOSEPH MARK - b. 1 Apr 1969; s/o Bradley Kent & Susan Buder (Horan) Garlinghouse.

JOSEPH MARK - b. 11 Mar 1972, Sault Ste. Marie, MI; s/o Jerry Louis & Ruby Mary (Long) Garlinghouse.

JOSEPH MILTON - b. 6 Oct 1856, Allens Hill, New York; d. 4 Jul 1882, Allens Hill, Ontario Co., New York; s/o John Nelson & Lucy West (Bothwell) Garlinghouse.

JOSEPH WILLIAM - b. 20 Jun 1991, Newport News, VA; s/o William John & Judy (Glascock) Garlinghouse.

JOSEPHINE "Rose" O. (McFadden) - b. 28 Jul 1856, IN; d. 9 Sep 1877, Allensville, Switzerland Co., IN; m. John Francis Oscar Garlinghouse 27 Aug 1870, Jefferson Co., IN, one child Charles "Charley" W.

JOSIAH - b. 27 Jun 1807; d. 1 Sep 1885, Isanti, Minn; s/o James L. & Susannah (Belknap) Garlinghouse. m. Amanda (Belknap) 1827, KY, children Catherine, Lacy, Susannah "Rosanna", James Mitchell, Mary, Rachel and Henry.

JOSIAH - b. 1871, Minn; s/o Lacy & Elizabeth (McCormick) Garlinghouse. m. Olive (...).

JOSIE (Robison) - b. 1878; m. George B. Garlinghouse 18 Jan 1899, Montezuma Co., Colo, children Elnora, Wallace, Heggie and Vivian.

JOYCE - b. 1958; d/o Ray Alden & Donna Annalee (Hausler) Garlinghouse.

JOYCE E. - m. Kieth David Garlinghouse. Living at Scotts Mills, OR in 1996.

JOYCE E. - Living at Cottage Grove, OR. in 1996.

JOYCE IVA - b. 1930; d/o Ira Birchfield & Iva Mable (Abeare) Garlinghouse. m. Raymond Vern Rase 1952, children Oscar Raymond, Amy Lu and Lisa Jo.

JUANITA (...) - m. Earl Garlinghouse, 1934.

JUDY (Furman) - m. Ira W. Garlinghouse three children.

JUDY (Glascock) - m. William John Garlinghouse 19 Nov 1983, children Christopher Thomas and Joseph William.

JULIA ALLERTON (Stebbins) - b. 1874; d. 1960, Clinton, NY. Buried at Sunset Hill Cemetery, Clinton, NY; m. John Newton Garlinghouse 5 Dec 1900 at St. James Church, Clinton, NY one child Helen.

JULIA ANN - b. 11 Sep 1803, Richmond Twp., Ontario Co., New York; d. 24 Dec 1883, Naples, Ontario Co., New York; d/o Benjamin & Anne (Morehouse) Garlinghouse. m. James French 1825, children Barzillai, Sara, Horace, Benjamin and Harriette.

JULIA ANN - b. 4 May 1864, Wayne, Steuben Co., New York; d. 13 Aug 1871, Wayne Steuben Co., New York; d/o Daniel Benjamin & Sarah "Sally" (Margeson) Garlinghouse.

JULIA ANNIE (Alder) - b.7 Sep 1866, Kings Stanley, Gloucestershire, Eng; d. 5 May 1943, San Antonio, Bexar Co., TX; m. Lorenzo J. Fisk 21 Jan 1883, San Antonio, TX, one child Albert. m2nd. Walter Sheldon Garlinghouse 12 Mar 1884, Eagle Pass, TX, children Walter Sheldon, Jr., Clara "Carrie", Arthur Alder and Lily. m3rd. Charles Huston Smith 1903, Washington, D.C., one child Jennie.

JULIA C. (Stuart) - b. 5 Mar 1863, Kan; m. Acil E. Garlinghouse 18 Jul 1898, Roseburg, Douglas Co., Oregon.

JULIA ELLEN - b. 12 Oct 1851, Ohio; d. 5 Mar 1858, Van Buren Co., Iowa; d/o Silas & Margaret (Reid) Garlinghouse.

JULIE ANN - b. 12 Aug 1960; d/o Bruce Beebe & Vivian Dickinson (Kabler) Garlinghouse. m. Jack R. Ridl 4 May 1983.

JULIE ANNE (Haidish) - b. 5 Feb 1947; m. Webb Mark Garlinghouse, one child Katherine Elizabeth.

JULIE BETH - b. 10 Jun 1965, MI; d/o Robert Vernon & Lorna May (Wagner) Garlinghouse.

JULIETTE - b. 1822; d/o James L. & Susannah (Belknap) Garlinghouse. m. Samuel Ulry 3 Mar 1842, Franklin Co., Ohio.

JUNIOR ELLSWORTH - b. 1925; s/o Elton Ellsworth & Leona (Beckman) Garlinghouse. m. Lucy (Gascho) 1942, children Gary Gene, Peggy Jean, John Ellsworth, Lucy Mae and Amber Joy.

JUSTIN ASA - b. 1979; s/o Kent Nelson & Rosemary (Gutierrez) Garlinghouse.

J. W. - s/o ... Garlinghouse. m. Mary Elizabeth (Harmon).

KAREN LYNN - b. 18 Sep 1963, Sault Ste. Marie, Mich; d/o Jerry Louis & Ruby Mary (Long) Garlinghouse.

KATHERINE - d/o Jennings Woodrow "Woodie" & Jeanne (...) Garlinghouse.

KATHERINE ELIZABETH - b. 16 Feb 1883, Vernon, Sussex Co., NJ; d. 2 Feb 1977; d/o John Monroe & Jesteen D. (Farber) Garlinghouse. m. Frank A. Forgerson 6 Mar 1902. m2nd. William Stremlaw. m3rd. ... Spangenberg "Spandenberg".

KATHERINE ELIZABETH - b. 11 Jun 1983; d/o Webb Mark & Julie Anne (Haidish) Garlinghouse.

KATHERINE MABEL (Fogwell) - b. 16 Mar 1881, Burlingame Twp., Kan; d. 1954, Topeka, Kan; m. Lewis Fayette Garlinghouse 4 Sep 1907, children Wendell Lewis and Francis Mark.

KATHERINE MONROE - b. 24 Dec 1980; d/o Richard Earl, Jr. & Margaret Ann (Pettys) Garlinghouse.

KATHLEEN - b. 28 Mar 1952; d/o Arnet John & Jean (Stewart) Garlinghouse. m. David Helm 20 Mar 1983, Billingham, Wash.

KATHRINE MARIE MORGAN - b. 12 May 1986, Berkeley, CA; d/o Robert Bruce & Diana (Morgan) Garlinghouse.

KATHRYN (Blanchard) - b. 1931; m. Royal Edsel Garlinghouse 1950, children Sharon Kay, David Royal, Lynn Marie and Steven Royal.

KATHY ANN - b. 6 Nov 1958, MI; d/o Robert Vernon & Lorna May (Wagner) Garlinghouse.

KATHY ANN - b. 14 Aug 1963, Sault Ste. Marie. Mich; d/o Frederick Mark & Doris Margaret (Long) Garlinghouse.

KAY (Rorck) - m. James Russell Garlinghouse, children Marc and Monica.

KEITH DAVID - b. 1962, Boulder, Colo; s/o Grant Wesley & Barbara Irene (Frame) Garlinghouse. m. Joyce E. (...). Livings at Scotts Mills, OR in 1996.

KELLY (...) - m. Matt Garlinghouse. Living at Fargo, ND 1996.

KENNETH - Living at Sault Ste. Marie, MI in 1996.

KENT - m.
Donna R. (...). Living at Alexandria, Minn in 1996.

KENT ARMIN - b. Great Falls, Mont; s/o Bruce Edmund Garlinghouse. m. Donna Jeannette (Falk) Aug 1967, one child Matthew Aaron.

KENT NELSON - b. 19 May 1950, Rockville Center, Nassau Co., New York; s/o Nelson Asa & Helen Matilda (Vossbrinck) Garlinghouse. m. Rosemary (Gutierrez) 12 Sep 1971, children Jason, Amanda Rose and Justin Asa.

KEVIN - m. D. (...). Living at Sault Ste. Marie, MI in 1996.

KEVIN MICHAEL - b. 22 Oct 1992, Lawrenceville, GA; s/o Walter Sheldon, III & Donna Marie (Schwieter) Garlinghouse.

KIMBERLY ANN - b. 15 Nov 1977, Paradise, CA; d/o Lester David & Diane Lynn (Bernard)

Garlinghouse.

KIMBERLY ANNE - b. 9 Mar 1966; d/o Bradley Kent & Susan Buder (Horan) Garlinghouse.

KIZIAH - b. @ 1785, NJ; possible d/o Stephen Gardenhouse (sic). m. Garrett Decker 10 Dec 1804, Amity, New York. She was niece of Kiziah Simmonson of Warwick, Orange Co., NY, a widow, who d. in 1796.

L. - m. Rick Loren Garlinghouse. Living at Auburn, MI in 1996.

LACY - b. 1830, Licking Co., Ohio; d. 21 Oct 1871, Mille Lacs Co., Minn; He served during the Civil War from 3 Sep 1862 to 4 Sep 1865 as Private in Company B of the 36th Regiment, Iowa Volunteer Infantry. s/o Josiah & Amanda (Belknap) Garlinghouse. m. Mary Jane (Belknap) 1855, Wapello Co., Iowa. m2nd. Elizabeth (McCormick) 18 Dec 1856, Blakesburg, Iowa, children Henry, Viola, Josiah, Ida, Rhoda, Cynthia and Esther A.

LACY - s/o ...Garlinghouse. Living at Sault Ste. Marie, MI in 1996.

LACY - s/o Henry & Eliza (...) Garlinghouse.

LACY GRANT - b. 11 Jan 1910, Kinross, Chippewa Co., Mich; d. May 1986, Saulte Ste. Marie, Chippewa Co., Mich; s/o Ulysses Grant Garlinghouse. m. Ruby Ella (Colwell) 31 May 1941, Sault Ste. Marie, Mich, children Dwayne Grant and Dean George.

LANAH (Brown) - m. Lorenzo Clay Garlinghouse 30 Jan 1890, Jefferson Co., IN.

LARRY - b. 30 Mar 1933; d. May 1985, Spokane, Wash; s/o Gerald Gilbert Garlinghouse. one child Gerald.

LARRY - b. 1962; s/o Eugene Wayne & Bonnie (Crumback) Garlinghouse.

LARRY - s/o ...Garlinghouse. m. Rebecca D. (...). Living at Odessa, TX in 1996.

LAURA - b. 30 Apr 1819, Richmond, Ontario Co., New York; d. 27 Aug 1820, Richmond, New York; d/o Joseph & Submit (Sheldon) Garlinghouse.

LAURA (Newman) - m. Franklin Garlinghouse, children Male, Ethel Mary and a stillborn.

LAURA ANN - b. 1950: d/o Lyle Rapheil & Elizabeth (Cemer) Garlinghouse.

LAURA ELMA (Hayden) - d. B/4 1923; m. Almond Jewett Garlinghouse 29 Jun 1892, one child Harold Charles.

LAURA M (Vancleave) - b. @ 1843, Iowa; m. John Andrew Garlinghouse 27 Oct 1878, Wapello Co., Iowa, children Elsa G., Female, b. 1884, Male, b. 1888 and George M.

LAVEY - b. 5 Mar 1906, Ohio; d. 17 Jan 1989, Beverly Hills, Los Angeles Co., CA; d/o Reid & Sue E. "Lou" (Miller) Garlinghouse.

LAWRENCE EDWIN - b. 2 Dec 1936; s/o Lester Edwin & Gladys Grace (Taylor) Garlinghouse. m. Genevieve E. (McClory) 23 May 1966, children Marie "Meg" E. and Lawrence Edwin.

LAWRENCE EDWIN - b. 19 Apr 1969; s/o Lawrence Edwin & Genevieve E. (McClory) Garlinghouse.

LAYMAN - b. 26 Apr 1893, Arcade, New York; d. 12 Sep 1893, Bennington, New York; s/o Arthur L. & Sarah M. (Baker) Garlinghouse.

LEE - m. Homer Garlinghouse, Living at Lebanon, OR in 1996.

LELAND EUGENE - b. @ 1890, Ohio; s/o William E. & Luella (Crego) Garlinghouse.

LELAND EUGENE - b. 20 Aug 1911, Delaware Co., Ohio; d. Oct 26 1983, San Francisco, CA; s/o Earl Leo & Oral C. (Whitney) Garlinghouse. m.

Betty Lois (Bone).

LELE EFAGENIA - b. 25 May 1880, TX; d. 15 Oct 1881, TX; d/o Cyrus Buell, Jr. & Amelia Florence (Fitzpatrick) Garlinghouse.

LEMAN BENTON - b. 16 Jan 1814, Canandaigua, Ontario Co., New York; d. 24 Jul 1872, Canandaigua, Ontario Co., New York; s/o Joseph & Submit (Sheldon) Garlinghouse. m. Martha Ann (Spalding) 19 Mar 1841, Lockport, Erie Co., New York, children Charles A., Amelia S., Arthur L., Frederick Leman, William Edward, Walter Sheldon, Caroline and Holmes Spalding.

LENORA REGINA - b. 4 Oct 1861, Van Buren Co., Iowa; d. Apr 1938, Wichita Falls, TX; d/o Andrew Leonard & Sarah Ann (Ratcliff) Garlinghouse. m. John Lemuel Moore, Sr. 22 Jun 1879, one child John Lemuel "Manny."

LENORE (...) - m. Anthony Garlinghouse.

LEO C. - b. Jan 1833; d. 17 Mar 1833, Burdett, Schuyler Co., New York; s/o Isaac Ashton & Hattie (Cory) Garlinghouse.

LEON - b. 1883; d. 1888; s/o Sherman Fayette & Mattie (Cheatham) Garlinghouse.

LEON - b. Prob. Globe, Ariz; s/o William L. Garlinghou5e.

LEON - s/o Mark & Elizabeth Victoria (Pope) Garlinghouse.

LEON "LEMAN" B. - b. 29 Mar 1892, Arcade, New York; He served during WW I as Private in the US Army; s/o Arthur L. & Sarah M. (Baker) Garlinghouse.

LEONA (Beckman) - m. Elton Ellsworth Garlinghouse 1923, children Junior Ellsworth,

Lyle Rapheil, Royal Edsel, Ralph Basil and Barbara Leigh.

LEONA M. - b. Oct 1865, Kan; d. 1940, Homer, Mich; Buried in Fairview Cem., Homer, Mich. d/o Abraham "Abram" & Agnes A. (Rose) Garlinghouse. m. William Waterman 1884, one child Jessie E

LEONA MAE (Beebe) - b. 25 Sept 1887, Tipton, Mich; d. 26 Jun 1937, Lansing, Ingham Co., Mich; m. Arnet John Garlinghouse 22 Oct 1910, Tipton, Mich., children Arnet John, Jr. and Bruce Beebe.

LEONARD - b. @ 1800, Ontario Co., New York; s/o John & Jane (Leonard) Garlinghouse.

LEONARD - b. 30 Dec 1905, Montezuma, Colo; d. 14 Mar 1906, Delores, Montezuma Co., Colo; s/o Elias B. & Virda Ellen (Lucas) Garlinghouse.

LEONARD A. - See ANDREW LEONARD.

LEONARD DEAL - b. 24 Dec 1906, Allen's Hill, Ontario Co., New York; d. 9 Oct 1950, Allen's Hill, Ontario Co., New York; Buried in St. Paul's Churchyard, Allen's Hill, New York. s/o Stoughton Tracy & Mary Henrietta (Deal) Garlinghouse. m. Elsie Sophia (Heberger) Chase 15 Apr 1936. He was a New York State Civil Engineer and he served in the military during WW II.

LEROY - b. Dec 1883, IN; d. 1936; s/o Sylvester R. & Lizzie White (Casebeer) Garlinghouse. m. Mary Ada (Ponton), one child Earl.

LESLIE - s/o Ulysses Grant Garlinghouse.

LESLIE - Living at Olathe, CO in 1996.

LESLIE H. - Living at Paris, Tenn in 1996.

LESLIE HOLMES, Sr. - b. Oct 1887, Leadville, Colo; d. 1953, Pasadena, CA; s/o Holmes Spalding & Emma Permelia (Sherman) Garlinghouse. m. Elsie Lee (Armstrong), children Leslie Holmes, Jr. and Lucy Lee. m2nd. Marybelle (Price) High 1947, Pasadena, CA. m3rd. Marjorie (Mason) Johnson after 1949, Laguna Beach, CA.

LESLIE HOLMES, JR. - b. 29 Jan 1914, Cleveland, Cuyahoga Co., Ohio; s/o Leslie Holmes & Elsie Lee (Armstrong) Garlinghouse, Sr. m. Elizabeth Amy Westfall (Soults) 1 Apr 1938, children Leslie Homer, Roland Edgar and Susan Lee.

LESLIE HOMER - b. 5 Mar 1941, Pasadena, CA; s/o Leslie Holmes & Elizabeth Amy Westfall (Soults) Garlinghouse, Jr. m. Estela (del Pozo) 27 Sep 1964.

LESTER - s/o ...Garlinghouse. Living at Magalia, CA in 1996.

LESTER DAVID - b. 7 Sep 1945, Chahalis, Wash; s/o Sherman Grant & Deloris Patricia (Shotts) Garlinghouse. m. Diane Lynn (Bernard) 12 Oct 1974, children Jennifer Lynn and Kimberly Ann.

LESTER EDWIN - b. 29 Jul 1912, Halfway, Oregon; s/o Lyman Edwin & Ida May (Spaulding) Garlinghouse. m. Gladys Grace (Taylor) 8 Feb 1936, Salem, Oregon, children Lawrence Edwin and Ellen Jane. m2nd. Mildred (...).

LETITIA "LATITIA" - b. 1844, Hart Co., KY; d/o George & Elcy Lee (Drury) Garlinghouse.

LETTIE "VIOLETTA" - b. 1847, MI; d. 1892; d/o David & Margaret Jane (Coryell) Garlinghouse. m. Henry F. Cogswell 1882, children Carrie Lulu and Jennie Vialettie.

LEVI CURTIS - b. 27 Sep 1852, IN; d. 27 Feb

1913, Madison, Jefferson Co., IN; s/o George Bennett & Isabella Jolly (DeWitt) Garlinghouse. m. Eva (Stuart) 1 Aug 1876, children Alice, Irene and Edna. m2nd. Ellen (Landers) 16 Mar 1899.

LEWANNA "LOUANNA" (Bennett) - b. about 1792, Benton, Ontario Co., NY; d. 7 Sep 1866, Madison, IN; m. John G. Garlinghouse about 1809, New York, children David Woodruff, Cyrus Buell, Submit S., Benjamin, George Bennett, Thomas Briggs, Lucy Irene and Andrew Leonard.

LEWANNA "LOVINA" - b. 1846, Van Buren, Co., Iowa; d/o Cyrus & Cassiah "Keziah" (Nichols) Garlinghouse. m. Joseph M. Kirkham 21 Mar 1866, Spencer Co., IN.

LEWIS FAYETTE - b. 8 Mar 1879, Shawnee Co., Kan; d. Dec 1965, Topeka, Kan; s/o Lucian Bonaparte & Matilda Ruth (Hanawalt) Garlinghouse. m. Katherine Mabel (Fogwell) 4 Sep 1907, children Wendell Lewis and Francis Mark.

LEWIS N. - b. 6 Dec 1837, Delaware Co., Ohio; d. 6 Dec 1911, National Military Home, Leavenworth, Kan; He served during the Civil War from 17 Jul 1861 to 30 Jul 1864 as Private in Company H, 5th Iowa Infantry. He was P.O.W. at Andersonville, GA. from 15 Feb 1864 to 15 Mar 1864. He was paroled at City Point, VA. He died on his 75th birthday. s/o Silas & Margaret (Reid) Garlinghouse. m. Nancy Jane "Jennie" (Lockerman) 4 Oct 1868, near Emporia, Lyon Co., Kan, children Owen Walter, Bertha May and Dora Maud.

LILLIAN (...) m. Peter Lynn Garlinghouse.

LILLY M. (Grady) - b., Owensboro, KY; m. Franklin Bennett Garlinghouse 27 Nov 1896, Spencer Co., IN, children Helen D., Aurelius DeWitt and Anna.

LILY - b. 1888, Ft. Clark, Kinney Co., TX; d. 1969, San Antonio, Bexar Co., TX; d/o Walter Sheldon & Julia Annie (Alder) Garlinghouse. m. William B. Carr 8 May 1908.

LINCINA "LUCINA" - b. 1828, New York; d/o Stephen A. & Elizabeth "Betsy" (Roberts) Garlinghouse.

LINDA (...) - m. Michael Garlinghouse. Living at Murphysboro, IL in 1996.

LINDA - d/o George William & Florence (Schultz) Garlinghouse. m. ... Blanchard, children Dick, Donna and Dianne.

LINDA MAE - b. 4 Aug 1954, Webb Co., TX; d/o Ralph Basil & Consuelo Hilda (Ramerz) Garlinghouse.

LIZZIE WHITE (Casebeer) - b. 1863-64, Mansfield, Ohio; d. 1927, Hillsdale, Vermillion Co., IN; m. Sylvester R. Garlinghouse 21 Feb 1883, Vermillion Co., IN, children LeRoy, Hugh A., Silvie M. and Georgia May.

LOIS E. - b. Oct 1878, CA; d/o Stephen & Prudence W. (Howard) Sanders Garlinghouse.

LOIS JANE - b. 14 Feb 1938, Madison, IN; d/o George Howard & Mildred (Jones) Garlinghouse. m. ... Turner.

LOLA (Martens) - m. Edward Joseph Garlinghouse.

LONNIE - Living at Tumwater, WA.

LOREN - s/o ... Garlinghouse. m. Marilyn (...). Living at Pinconning, MI in 1996.

LOREN IRA - b. 1929; s/o Ira Burchfield & Iva Mable (Abeare) Garlinghouse. m. Patricia Ann

(Spaulding) 1951, children Rick Loren and Cynthia Ann.

LORENZO CLAY - b. 22 Oct 1864, Allensville, Switzerland Co., IN; d. 11 Jun 1908, Madison, Jefferson Co., IN; s/o George Bennett & Serena Milton Boyd (Crusan) Garlinghouse. m. Reginia (de Bando) 10 Feb 1887, Jefferson Co., In. m2nd. Lanah (Brown) 30 Jan 1890, Jefferson Co., IN. m3rd. Serelda Catherine (Ashley) 12 Sep 1894, Jefferson Co., IN, children Serelda Catherine and Sarah Jeannette.

LORI (...) - m. ... Garlinghouse. Living at Saulte Ste. Marie, MI in 1996.

LORINDA (Short) - b. @ 1811; d. 13 Dec 1849, Richmond, Ontario Co., New York; Buried in St. Paul's Churchyard, Allen's Hill, Ontario Co., New York. m. John Nelson Garlinghouse 24 May 1836, children Arabella "Belle" Louise and Jane "Jennie" Delphine.

LORNA MAY (Wagner) - m. Robert Vernon Garlinghouse 6 Jan 1952, children Sandra Kay, Robert Craig, Kathy Ann, Gerald Lloyd and Julie Beth.

LORRAINE (Fredericks) - m. Albert Edward Garlinghouse, children Frederick and Carol.

LOUIS EDWARD - b. 23 Nov 1928, Madison, IN; s/o George Howard & Mildred (Jones) Garlinghouse. m. Eva (Mahoney), one child Gail Elaine.

LOUISA - b. 7 Feb 1835, NJ; d/o Joseph & Maria "Mary" (Ryerson) Garlinghouse. m. Alfred Nichols 22 Jul 1860, High Street Presbyterian Church, Newark, NJ.

LOUISE - b. 1848, Ohio; d/o Thomas Briggs & Augusta (Demmett) Garlinghouse.

LOUISE (Hess) - b. Nov 1875; d. 1932; Buried in

Fairview Cem., Homer, Mich. m. Charly "Charles" Abram Garlinghouse 20 Sep 1892, Calhoun Co., Mich, children Bryan Hess and Viola L.

LOUISE (...) - m. Robert Garlinghouse. Living at Sterling Heights, MI in 1996.

LOUISE A. - b. 15 Jun 1823, Richmond, Ontario Co., New York; d. 25 Aug 1890, LeRoy, New York; d/o Joseph & Submit (Sheldon) Garlinghouse. m. Maj. William Harold Sheldon 14 Oct 1846, Avon, New York, children Walter G. and Harriet "Hattie" J.

LOVILLA GERTRUDE - b. 1924; d/o Ira Birchfield & Iva Mable (Abeare) Garlinghouse. m. Harold Lloyd Miller 1941, children Harold Ira, Ronald Lee and Bonnie Lou.

LOVINA "SAVINA" - b. 1 Dec 1839, White Co., IN; d. 4 Dec 1918, Lovington, IL; d/o David Woodruff & Grace (Mitchell) Garlinghouse. m. George L. Alexander Hout 10 Nov 1861, Effingham Co., IL, children Wesley, Harmon, William S. and Sherman M. m2nd. Matthew R. Call 1869, children Nancy M., Martha B., David G. and Mary Jane.

LUCIAN BONAPARTE - b. 26 Apr 1844, Licking Co., Ohio; d. 16 Jan 1907; Buried at Centre Village, Ohio; s/o George & Sophronia (Sherman) Garlinghouse. m. Matilda Ruth (Hanawalt) Garlinghouse, children Elbannis Carroll, Orestes Lucian, Ina Bell, Almina Tillie, George Lovette, Lewis Fayette and Nellie Amelia.

LUCIAN CLARK - b. 19 Apr 1907, Kan; d. 8 Jul 1908; s/o Orestes Lucian, M.D. & Pearl Amy (Clark) Garlinghouse.

LUCRETIA D. - b. 1852-54, Wapello Co., Iowa; Buried at Alexander, ND, as "Grandma Jarvis"; d/o David Woodruff & Catherine (Garlinghouse)

Garlinghouse. m. Frank P. Carothers 17 Apr 1867, Wapello Co., Iowa. m2nd. Lott Hilton 31 May 1871, Princeton, Minn, children Allen, Gladys, Agnes, Mary, Dorothy, Homer Allen and John Herbert. m3rd. ... Anderson, one child George. m4th. ... Jarvis.

LUCY - b. Feb 1860; d. 23 Apr 1922; d/o David B. & Mary A. (Davis) Garlinghouse. m. ... Barrett.

LUCY - b. 1869, Pueblo, Pueblo Co., Colo; d/o Andrew Leonard & America J. (Bradburn) Garlinghouse.

LUCY - b. 1871, Minn; d/o Henry & Eliza (...) Garlinghouse.

LUCY (Gascho) - b. 1926; m. Junior Ellsworth Garlinghouse 1942, children Gary Gene, Peggy Jean, John Ellsworth, Lucy Mae and Amber Joy.

LUCY A. (...) - m. Hazel "Hec" "Hasel" Rupert Garlinghouse.

LUCY EMELINE (Ludy) - b. 1830, New York; m. Thomas Garlinghouse 25 Sep 1871, Washtenaw Co., Mich, one child Samuel.

LUCY LEE - b. 1918, Berkeley, San Marino Co., CA; d/o Leslie Holmes & Elsie Lee (Armstrong) Garlinghouse. m. Walter Franklin Dexter, Sr., children Walter Franklin, Jr. and Daniel.

LUCY LIVINGS - b. 4 Oct 1870, IN; d. 1965, Rockport, IN; d/o Aurelius DeWitt & Mary "Mollie" (deBruler) Garlinghouse. m. John E. Taylor 19 Apr 1893, Spencer Co., IN, one child Townsend John.

LUCY MAE - b. 1955; d/o Junior Ellsworth & Lucy (Gascho) Garlinghouse.

LUCY WEST (Bothwell) - b. 8 Sep 1825, Scotland;

d. 25 Feb 1905, Allen's Hill, Ontario Co., New York; Buried in St. Paul's Churchyard, Allen's Hill, New York. m. John Nelson Garlinghouse 15 Oct 1853, children Abigail Mary, Joseph Milton, Nellie Bothwell, Emma L., Stoughton Tracy, Adelaide "Addie" E. and Fanny B.

LUELLA (Crego) - b. about 1865; m. William E. Garlinghouse 2 Dec 1885, Delaware Co., Ohio, children Earl Leo, Leland Eugene and Howard.

LUKE JOHN - b. 14 May 1975, Sault Ste Marie, Mich; s/o Frederick Mark & Doris Margaret (Long) Garlinghouse.

LULU E. - b. 18 Nov 1873, Tecumseh, Lenawee Co., Mich; d. 15 Oct 1893, Tecumseh, Lenawee Co., Mich; d/o Daniel Benjamin & Carrie (Wolcott) Garlinghouse.

LYDIA "LIDDA" - b. 1872, Hillsdale, Vermillion Co., IN; d/o Cyrenus A. & Sarah A. (Jackson) Garlinghouse. m. Will E. McLaughlin 27 Sep 1891, Vermillion Co., IN, one child Don.

LYLE DAVID - b. @ 1950, Albion, NY; d. 20 July 1995, Groveland, FL; s/o Delmar & Lynn "Evelyn" (Sargent) Garlinghouse. m. Barbara L. (Owens) one child Tracy Lynn.

LYLE RAPHEIL - b. 1926; s/o Elton Ellsworth & Leona (Beckman) Garlinghouse. m. Elizabeth (Cemer) 1944, children Laura Ann, Debra Lynn and Penny Sue.

LYMAN EDWIN - b. 16 May 1872, Sand Springs, Iowa; d. 29 Mar 1961, Boise, Idaho; s/o Darius Hill & Minerva Jane "Jennie" (White) Garlinghouse. m. Nellie Littlefield 6 Mar 1896. m2nd. Ida May (Spaulding) 1 Apr 1908, Portland, Oregon, children Margaret, Gordon Spaulding, Lester Edwin and Ace Nelson.

LYNN (Hartman) - m. Fayette Garlinghouse 28 Jan

1916.

LYNN "Evelyn" (Sargent). m. Delmar Garlinghouse one child Lyle David.

LYNN - b. 1937, Lewiston, Idaho; d/o Richard Lynn Garlinghouse. m. ... Reid, one child Seanna.

LYNN - d/o Jeremiah "Gerald" & Bessie (...) Garlinghouse.

LYNN MARIE - b. 1957; d/o Royal Edsel & Kathryn (Blanchard) Garlinghouse.

MABEL (Flood) - b. 8 Dec 189?, Vernon, Sussex Co., NJ; d. 1 Jun 1940, Vernon, NJ; m. Vernon Garlinghouse, children Margaret and Vernon.

MABEL (...) - m. Richard Garlinghouse 1961.

MABEL - d/o John Francis Oscar & Mary E. (McClure) Garlinghouse. m. Walter Gams.

MABLE (...) - m. Ulysses Grant Garlinghouse.

MANGNIA ELIZABETH - b. 17 Jun 1914, Hillsdale, Vermillion Co., IN; d/o Hugh A. & Eva O. (Watson) Garlinghouse.

MARC - s/o James Russell & Kay (Rorck) Garlinghouse.

MARCIA - b. 1768; d. 17 Nov 1845, Naples, Ontario Co., New York; Buried in Barker Church Cem., Italy Valley Road, Italy, Yates Co., New York. Prob. d/o James & Joanna (Buchanan) Garlinghouse.

MARGARET (Reid) - b. 12 Feb 1812, PA; d. 14 Jan 1899, Winfield, Kan; m. Silas Garlinghouse 1 Nov 1832, Delaware, Ohio, children William, Melissa Eliza, Calista Emily, Lewis N., Stephen, Arthelia Jane, George, Rhodelia Ann, Norman Fayette, Alta Maria, Julia Ellen, Hiram and Martha Elizabeth.

MARGARET (Bloom) - m. Almond Jewett Garlinghouse 1923.

MARGARET (Stephenson) - m. George Howard Garlinghouse 1918, one child Inez Florence.

MARGARET (Hammer) - d. 1963; m. Oscar Ross Garlinghouse 30 Nov 1926, one child Edwin Oscar.

MARGARET - b. 1908; d. 1909; d/o Lyman Edwin & Ida May (Spaulding) Garlinghouse.

MARGARET - b. 21 Apr 1914; d. 2 Nov 1918; d/o Edward Sylvester & Emma (Shae) Garlinghouse.

MARGARET - d/o Vernon & Mabel (Flood) Garlinghouse. m. Edward ""Red"" Guthrie.

MARGARET (Pettys) - b. 9 Jun 1943; m. Richard Earl Garlinghouse, Jr. 23 Sep 1972, children Sarah McCall, Elizabeth Clark and Katherine Monroe.

MARGARET (...) - m. Rick Garlinghouse. Living at Auburn, MI in 1996.

MARGARET - d/o Dean George & Gretta (...) Garlinghouse.

MARGARET C. (Gray) - b. 1870, Mich; d. @ 1917; m. Benson J. Garlinghouse 26 Nov 1895, Mich, children Burton A. and John G. m2nd. Homer C. Brewer 24 Nov 1915, Detroit, Wayne Co., Mich.

MARGARET JANE (Coryell) - b. 21 May 1809, NY; d. 17 Oct 1862, Napoleon, MI; m. David Garlinghouse 1831, Steuben Co., New York, children Ira Reed, John Coryell, Daniel Benjamin, Lettie "Violetta" and a daughter who died as an infant.

MARGARET L. (Black) - b. 1858; d. 1898, Mich; m. William Eighney; m2nd. Adelbert E. Garlinghouse 6 Apr 1892, Erie Twp., Monroe Co., Mich.

MARGARET "Peggy" LEE - b. 1928, Los Angeles, CA; d/o Albert Frederick & Ferne Beatrice

(Armstrong) Garlinghouse. m. Donald Monfort Sperry 1951, San Marino, CA, children David Ralph and Katherine Ferne.

MARGARET LEE - b. 1941; d/o Vernon Lloyd & Margaret Lillian (Kaufman) Garlinghouse. m. Leonard Butler 1959, children Daniel Leonard, John Vernon, Leonard Warren, Annette Lee and Dawn Marie.

MARGARET LILLIAN (Kaufman) - m. Vernon Lloyd Garlinghouse 1928, children Robert Vernon, Eugene Wayne and Margaret Lee.

MARGUERITE (McNair) - b. 22 Sep 1899; d. Apr 1933, Potomac, MD; m. ... Devers. m2nd. Albert Frederick Garlinghouse 1951, Eagle Rock, CA.

MARIA "Mary" (Ryerson) - b. 22 Nov 1791, Two Bridges, NJ; d. 9 Jun 1857, Newark, NJ; m. Joseph Garlinghouse 5 Jul 1811, Pompton, NJ, children Mary, Eliza, Ellen, Catherine, John and Louise.

MARIA - b. 17 Feb 1803, NJ; d/o Thomas & Polly "Mary" (Benjamin) Garlinghouse.

MARIAH "MARIA" - b. 1853, Van Buren Co., Iowa; d/o Cyrus Buell & Cassiah "Keziah" (Nichols) Garlinghouse. m. Christopher W. Swain 13 Nov 1873, Parke Co., IN.

MARIAN - Living at Lebanon, OR in 1996.

MARIE "MEG" - b. 8 Feb 1967; d/o Lawrence Edwin & Genevieve E. (McClory) Garlinghouse.

MARIE (Parker) - m. Vernon Garlinghouse, children Cindy and Debbie.

MARIE S. (...) m. ..., m2nd Frederick Samuel Garlinghouse.

MARJIE - b. 1908-9, Lewiston, Idaho; d/o Gerald

Arza & Elizabeth (Gilbert) Garlinghouse. m. ... Farrish.

MARJORIE (Mason) - m. ... Johnson. m2nd. Leslie Holmes Garlinghouse after 1949, Laguna Beach, CA.

MARJORIE COSPER (Beard) - b. 16 Jul 1915; m. Francis Mark Garlinghouse 18 Nov 1939, children Bradley Kent, Webb Mark and Whitney Beard.

MARJORIE ELISE - b. 27 Nov 1967; d/o Bradley Kent & Susan Buder (Horan) Garlinghouse.

MARJORIE PEARL - b. 25 Jul 1900, Kan; d/o Orestes Lucian, M.D. & Pearl Amy (Clark) Garlinghouse. m. Spencer A. Gard, one child Amy Lou.

MARK - b. 1 Jul 1903, Kinross, Chippewa Co., MI; d. 17 Jun 1957, Kinross, Chippewa Co., MI; s/o Ulysses Grant Garlinghouse. m. Elizabeth Victoria (Pope) 11 Apr 1933, Sault Ste. Marie, MI, children Frederick Mark, Jerry Louis, Donald, Diane Elizabeth, Leon, Bradley Gene and Randy John.

MARK - s/o Herbert Hoover & Mary Lou (...) Garlinghouse.

MARK SAMUEL - b. 13 Sep 1968, Sault Ste Marie, MI; s/o Frederick Mark & Doris Margaret (Long) Garlinghouse.

MARTHA "PATTY" - d/o James & Elanor "Eleanor" (Hunt) Garlinghouse. m. Rufus Palmer, children David, Daniel and Filina.

MARTHA - b. 1840; d/o George & Amelia (Webb) Garlinghouse.

MARTHA ANN (Spalding) - b. 5 Mar 1818, Rochester, Monroe Co., New York; d. 5 Oct 1882, Buffalo, Erie Co., New York; Buried in

Woodlawn Cem., Canandaigua, Ontario Co., New York m. Leman Benton Garlinghouse 2 Jun 1841, Lockport, Erie Co., New York, children Charles A., Amelia S., Arthur L., Frederick Leman, William Edward, Walter Sheldon, Caroline and Holmes Spalding.

MARTHA E. - b. 1836, Hart Co., KY; d/o George & Elcy Lee (Drury) Garlinghouse.

MARTHA ELIZABETH - b. 8 Apr 1855, Delaware Co., Ohio; d. 26 Jan 1897, Winfield, Kan; d/o Silas & Margaret (Reid) Garlinghouse.

MARTHA J. (Morris) - d. 8 Dec 1953; m. Willard Garlinghouse.

MARTIN LEROY "ROY" - b. 17 Nov 1924, Lewis, Montezuma Co., Colo; He served during World War II in the US Air Corps; s/o Elias Buell & Virda Ellen (Lucas) Garlinghouse. m. Anne Stark.

MARTIN V. - b. Sep 1840-45, Prob. Shelby Co., IN; d. 24 May 1903, Globe, Ariz; He served during the Civil War from 20 Apr 1861 to 5 Jan 1865 as Musician in Co. E, 50th Regiment of Indiana Volunteers; s/o Cyrus Buell & Cassiah "Keziah" (Nichols) Garlinghouse. m. Sarah Ann (Long) 28 Dec 1870, Augusta, Butler Co., Kan, children Minnie, Evalina Florence, Emma Kate, Cyrus Buell, III, Hattie and G.W.

MARY (Monroe) - b. 30 Apr 1782; d. 7 Jun 1847, Vernon, Sussex Co., NJ; Buried in the United Methodist Churchyard, Vernon, Sussex Co., NJ. m. Gamaliel Garlinghouse 1800, children Thomas, Mary, James, John, George, Hannah, Mary, David B. and Thomas D.

MARY - b. @ 1785; d/o ... Gardinghous (sic). m. Christopher Sindal 2 Oct 1805, Essex Co., NJ.

MARY - b. 19 Jun 1797, Springwater, Ontario

Co., New York; She was first white child born in Springwater, New York. d. 15 Jun 1869, Richmond, Ontario Co., New York; d/o John & Jane (Leonard) Garlinghouse. m. Thomas Briggs, Richmond, New York, children Leonard B. and Barzillai T.

MARY - b. 17 Feb 1803, Vernon, Sussex Co., NJ; d. young; d/o Gamaliel & Mary (Monroe) Garlinghouse.

MARY - b. 4 Jul 1817, NJ; d. 20 Nov 1899, Newark, NJ; d/o Joseph & Maria "Mary" (Ryerson) Garlinghouse. m. Cornelius H. Jacobus 11 May 1838, children Sarah, Augustus, Wallace, Emma, Ransford, Herman, Spencer, Anna, Mary Estelle, Amzi N. and Clarence.

MARY - b. 7 May 1821, Vernon, Sussex Co., NJ; d. 3 Jan 1901, Chester, NY; d/o Gamaliel & Mary (Monroe) Garlinghouse. m. Samuel Collard, children Thomas T., Hannah M., Caroline Ophelia, Sarah and Susan Feagles.

MARY (Margeson) - b. 21 Feb 1825, Sussex Co., NJ; d. 18 May 1853, Wayne, Steuben Co., New York; m. Daniel Benjamin Garlinghouse 27 Sep 1848, children Frank, Isaac Ashton and Mary Elizabeth.

MARY - b. 10 Jan 1826, Richmond, New York; d. 1917, Chicago, IL; d/o Joseph & Submit (Sheldon) Garlinghouse. m. Orville Comstock, one child Louise B.

MARY - b. 1836, Licking Co., Ohio; d. 1882; d/o Josiah & Amanda (Belknap) Garlinghouse. m. John Staples 27 Mar 1855, Foley, Benton Co., Minn., children Richard H., Clarence, John R., Cyrus S., Norris, Harriet, Alice V., Eugene and Herbert.

MARY - b. 1 May 1846; d. 1 May 1916; d/o George & Amelia (Webb) Garlinghouse. m. ...

Neiswender.

MARY "Mollie" (deBruler) - b. 18 Dec 1848, IN; d. Feb 1928; m. Aurelius DeWitt Garlinghouse 13 Dec 1869, Spencer Co., IN, children Lucy Livings and Franklin Bennett.

MARY (Berkland) - b. 1886, Chippewa Co., MI; d. 1969, Kinross, Chippewa Co., MI; m. Joseph Garlinghouse, Chippewa Co., MI, they had one child died young.

MARY "MAY" - d/o James & Anna (Bennet) Garlinghouse. m. ... Collins.

MARY A. (Davis) - b. 12 Jun 1832, Catskill, New York; d. 24 Nov 1905, Bellvale, Orange Co., New York; Buried in Warwick Cem., Warwick, New York. m. David B. Garlinghouse, children James, Lucy and Georgianna.

MARY ADA (Ponton) - b. 24 Jun 1892, Hillsdale, Vermillion Co., IN; m. LeRoy Garlinghouse, one child Earl.

MARY ANN "POLLY" - b. about 1790, prob. Luzerne Co., PA; d. 1867, Benton Co., Oregon; d/o James & Elanor "Eleanor" (Hunt) Garlinghouse. m. Jonas Newton Belknap, Jr. 15 Jan 1813, Ontario Co., New York, children Orin, Silas, Electa, Rachell and Eleanor.

MARY ANN (Jones) - b. 26 May 1829, KY; d. 3 Sep 1905, Monroe, Benton Co., OR; m. William Coyle. m2nd. William Garlinghouse 23 Sep 1885, Lane Co., OR.

MARY ANN - b. 23 Nov 1835, Richmond, Ontario Co., New York; d. 10 Apr 1916, Naples, Ontario Co., New York; d/o Samuel S. & Orpha (Harrington) Garlinghouse. m. Isaac Wilbur Wilcox 19 Aug 1857, Richmond, Ontario Co., New York, children Etheline Nora "Ella", Jessie Fremont, Ulric Delgreen, Mary Ann, Jennie Elvira, Orpha Adell and Ellen Linia.

MARY E. (Willits) - b. Apr 1848, Egypt, New York; d. 16 Jun 1906, Ann Arbor, Washtenaw Co., MI; m. Nelson S. Garlinghouse 17 Oct 1867, Ann Arbor, MI, children Ida E. and Frank W.

MARY E. (McClure) - b. about 1861, IN; m. John Francis Oscar Garlinghouse 15 Jan 1879, Madison, Jefferson Co., IN, children Bess, Mabel and Fred Bartlett.

MARY ELIZABETH (Hewitt) - b. @ 1843, Saratoga Co., New York; d. 17 Aug 1904, Rochester, Monroe Co., New York; Buried in Old Cem., Canandaigua, New York. m. Charles A. Garlinghouse 6 Dec 1866, Canandaigua, New York, one child Nettie.

MARY ELIZABETH (Seaton) - b. @ 1844; m. James Mitchell Garlinghouse 8 Aug 1863, Princeton, Mille Lacs Co., Minn. m2nd. Thomas Powell 28 Dec 1869, LaCrosse, LaCrosse Co., Wisc.

MARY ELIZABETH - b. 30 Apr 1853, Wayne, Steuben Co., New York; d. 21 Jul 1864, Wayne, Steuben Co., New York; d/o Daniel Benjamin & Mary (Margeson) Garlinghouse.

MARY ELIZABETH (Ashley) - b. 1 Jan 1873, Allensville, Switzerland Co., IN; d. 6 Dec 1941, Madison, Switzerland Co., IN; m. Willard Elmer Garlinghouse 8 Apr 1891, Jefferson, IN, children Florence Luanna, Ella Murat, Ida Elena and George Howard.

MARY ELIZABETH (Hermon) - b. 8 Apr 1914, CA; d. 27 Sep 1985, Humboldt, CA; m. J. W. Garlinghouse.

MARY ELLEN (Gilpatrick) - m. Frederick Leman Garlinghouse 3 Apr 1878, Saco, ME, one child Nanie.

MARY ERSKINE (Davis)- b. 19 Dec 1869, Madison,

Jefferson Co., IN; m. Ulysses Arthur Garlinghouse 20 Sep 1894, Madison, Jefferson Co., IN, children Nelda Lurada, Arlene Ruth and Henry Elmer Nathan.

MARY F. - b. 31 Jul 1856, Van Buren, Iowa; d. 13 Oct 1856, Van Buren, Iowa; Buried in White Chapel Cem., Lick Creek Twp., Van Buren Co., Iowa. d/o William & Elizabeth (Huff) Garlinghouse.

MARY GAIL (Bock) - m. Roland Edgar Garlinghouse 30 Jul 1966.

MARY HENRIETTA (Deal) - b. 10 Dec 1873; d. 12 Jan 1931, Allens Hill, Ontario Co., NY; m. Stoughton Tracy Garlinghouse, 22 Oct 1902, Allens Hill, NY. children Leonard Deal and Nelson Asa.

MARY INEZ (Hilliard) - b. 5 May 1890, Iowa; d. 28 May 1980, Pasadena, CA; Buried at Forest Lawn Mem. Pk., Glendale, CA. m. John Ulmont Garlinghouse.

MARY JANE (Wilson) - b. 22 Aug 1819; d. 11 Mar 1896, Napoleon, Lenawee Co., Mich; m. David Garlinghouse 16 Oct 1867, Somerset, Mich.

MARY JANE (Benedict) - b. 11 Feb 1827, Warwick, Orange Co., New York; d. 11 Nov 1901, Tecumseh, Lenawee Co., Mich; m. John Benedict Garlinghouse 10 Dec 1850, Warwick, Orange Co., New York, children Gurdon Benedict, Burton A. and Benson.

MARY JANE (Belknap) - b. 1830, Licking Co., Ohio; d. 1864; m. Lacy Garlinghouse 1855, Wapello Co., Iowa

MARY JANE - b. Feb 1842, White Co., IN; d Apr 1911, Bement, IL; Buried at Freemanton Cem., Effingham Co., IL. d/o David Woodruff & Grace (Mitchell) Garlinghouse. m. Henry Sinclair Redman 22 Nov 1860, Effingham Co., IL, children Travis, Evaline, Cornelius, Levina and Anthony.

MARY JEAN - b. 15 May 1939; d/o Robert Orestes, M.D. & Esther Winifred (Coghill) Garlinghouse. m. John Price Witwer 28 Dec 1968, children Robert Earl and Elizabeth Anne.

MARY L. - b. Mar 1878, Wapello Co., Iowa; d/o James H. Garlinghouse.

MARY LOU (...) - m. Herbert Hoover Garlinghouse, one child Mark.

MARY M. - b. 1869, Minn; d/o Henry & Eliza (...) Garlinghouse.

MARY MAY - b. 28 Aug 1908 Lebanon, Montezuma Co., Colo; d. 4 Jan 1959, St. Luke's Hosp., Denver, Colo; Buried in Crown Hill Cem. d/o Elias Buell & Virda Ellen (Lucas) Garlinghouse. m. Alva Schaaf 1929, one child LeRoy. m2nd. Floyd Arbuckle.

MARYBELLE (Price) - m. ... High. m2nd. Leslie Holmes Garlinghouse 1947, Pasadena, CA.

MARYLEN (...) - m. Chuck W. Garlinghouse.

MATILDA CECILE - b. 30 Nov 1908; d/o George Lovette & Cora (Oursler) Garlinghouse. m. Kenneth H. McGibben 18 Jun 1933, children Kendra, Kay and Karen.

MATILDA RUTH (Hanawalt) - b. 28 Feb 1845, Ohio; d. 2 Jun 1916; m. Lucian Bonaparte Garlinghouse 17 Nov 1867, Licking Co., Ohio, children Elbannis Carroll, Orestes Lucian, Ina Bell, Almina Tillie, George Lovette, Lewis Fayette and Nellie Amelia.

MATTHEW AARON - b. 16 Dec 1973; s/o Kent Armin & Donna Jeannette (Falk) Garlinghouse.

MATTHEW DAVID - b. 11 Oct 1975; s/o Bradley Kent & Susan Buder (Horan) Garlinghouse.

MATTIE (Cheatham) - b. 1856; d. 1884; m. Sherman Fayette Garlinghouse, children Valnor C. and Leon.

MAUDE (Williams) - b. 12 Feb 1888; d. Jan 1986, Brutus, Mich; m. Arnet John Garlinghouse 8 May 1941.

MAURICE - Living at Mount Vernon, IL. in 1996.

MAVIS - b. after 1880; d/o George C. & Hellin (...) Garlinghouse.

MELISSA (...) - m. Robert Garlinghouse. Living at Lebanon, OR in 1996.

MELISSA A. "Milicia" - b. 1846, Hart Co., KY; d/o George & Elcy Lee (Drury) Garlinghouse. m. George P. Cramer 21 Mar 1888, Albia, Monroe Co., Iowa.

MELISSA A. (Coryell) - b. Jul 1837, Mich; d. 3 May 1891, Mich; m. Ira Reed Garlinghouse 1856, children Adelbert E., John Edward, Etha and Anna E. "Anna May."

MELISSA ELIZA - b. 12 Nov 1834, Ohio; d. 29 Aug 1899, S. Omaha, Neb; d/o Silas & Margaret (Reid) Garlinghouse. m. Emanuel Cockerell 4 Jul 1854, Delaware Co., Ohio, children Nathan and Lewis.

MERVYN W. "Bud" - b. 9 Mar 1914, Ohio; d. 30 Jun 1987, Ostrander, Ohio; s/o Earl Leo & Oral C. (Whitney) Garlinghouse. m. Grace (...), children Donald L. and Carol.

MICHAEL - b. 1959; s/o Ray Alden & Donna Annalee (Hausler) Garlinghouse.

MICHAEL - Living at Murphysboro, IL in 1996.

MILDRED - b. 29 Feb 1894, Topeka, Shawnee Co., Kan; d. 9 Nov 1924, Donna, Hidalgo Co., TX; d/o Elbannis Carroll & Axie "Achsa" Mable (Yingling) Garlinghouse. m. ... McCullough.

MILDRED - d/o Earl Leo & Oral C. (Whitney) Garlinghouse. m. C. E. Zolman.

MILDRED (Jones) - b. 17 Jun 1906, Carrollton, KY; d. May 1973, Madison, Jefferson Co., IN; m. George Howard Garlinghouse 23 Feb 1924, children George "Billy" Willard, Betty Jo, Louis Edward, Nathan Andrew, Nancy Joyce, John Daniel and Lois Jane.

MILDRED (...) - m. Lester Edwin Garlinghouse. Living at Boise, ID in 1996.

MINERVA JANE "Jennie" (White) - b. 28 Dec 1845, Greenfield, Ohio; d. 17 Dec 1924, Sand Springs, Iowa; m. Darius Hill Garlinghouse 15 Dec 1863, Rockville, Iowa, children Jennie May, Emma Frank, Edmund Oscar, Almond Jewett, Lyman Edwin, Nelson Darius, Orpha Marie, Samuel Dayton, Jesse Mabel and Nina Grace.

MINNIE - b. 1874, Kan; d. B/4 13 Apr 1898; d/o Martin V. & Sarah Ann (Long) Garlinghouse.

MINNIE (Lee) - b. 1890, NC; d. 9 Oct 1923, Globe, Ariz; m. Cyrus Buell Garlinghouse about 1915, one child William L.

MINNIE (Baskwell) - m. Charles Oliver Garlinghouse 23 Sep 1877, Spencer Co., IN.

MINNIE L. (Divilbiss) - d. 11 Jun 1969, Wilbarger Co., TX; m. George Lovette Garlinghouse.

MINNIE MINERVA (Gates) - b. 3 Sept 1855; d. 26 Feb 1912, Tecumseh, Lenawee Co., Mich; m. Gurdon Benedict Garlinghouse, children Clarissa Maye, Ethalyn Virginia, Otto Gates, Arnet John and his twin who died in 1888.

MIRIAM (Thoroman) - b. 20 Feb 1909; m. Richard Earl Garlinghouse, M.D., children Richard Earl, Jr. and Gretchen Ann.

MONICA - d/o James Russell & Kay (Rorck) Garlinghouse.

MONONIA ELIZABETH - b. 17 Jun 1914, Hillsdale, Vermillion Co., IN; d/o Hugh A. & Eva O. (Watson) Garlinghouse.

MONROE - b. 3 Aug 1890, Vernon, Sussex Co., NJ; d. Dec 1964, NJ; s/o John Monroe & Jesteen D. (Farber) Garlinghouse. children Richard, Roy, Delmer and Ruth.

MORRIS - b. Jul 1885, Wash; s/o Norman Fayette "Frank" & Ada (...) Garlinghouse.

MORSE NOLAN - b. 1913, Clarkston, Wash; s/o Gerald Arza & Elizabeth (Gilbert) Garlinghouse. m. Dorothy Lillian (Roessell), children Jon Jay and Sandra.

MURIEL BEATRICE (Montgomery) - b. 13 Sep 1894, St. Louis, MO; d. 15 Oct 1957, Orlando, FL; Buried in Greenwood Cem., Orlando, FL. m. Arthur Alder Garlinghouse 2 Nov 1914, Puerto Rico, one child Arthur Alder, Jr.

MYRNA - b. about 1908, CA; d/o Orville & Violet (...) Garlinghouse.

NANCY - d/o Ira W. Garlinghouse.

NANCY ELIZABETH - b. 1922, Lihue, Hawaii; d/o Ralph Leman & Elizabeth Hayes (Davison) Garlinghouse. m. Hugh John Lowe, Jr. 1945, children Mary and Margaret. m2nd. Major Lloyd Bryan Dochterman 1958, Paris, France, one child Kristin Elizabeth.

NANCY JANE "Jennie" (Lockerman) - b. about 1849, IN or IL; d. B/4 3 Mar 1898; m. Lewis N. Garlinghouse 4 Oct 1868, near Emporia, Lyon Co., Kan, children Owen Walter, Bertha May and Dora Maud.

NANCY JEANNE - b. 1946, Aitkin Co., Minn; d/o Robert Erwin & Agnes (Oakland) Garlinghouse. m. Jerry Adams, children Patrick Michael and Thomas Mitchel. m2nd. Charles Provost.

NANCY JOYCE - b. 3 Mar 1934; d/o George Howard & Mildred (Jones) Garlinghouse. m. William E. Spillman, Jr. 18 Jun 1949, Madison, IN, one child Rhinda Sue

NANCY RUTH (Manus) - b. 16 Jul 1956, Frankfurt, Ger; m. Whitney Beard Garlinghouse, children James Manus, Whitney Christopher and Peter Mark.

NANIE - b. 1880, Kan; d. young; d/o Frederick Leman & Mary Ellen (Gilpatrick) Garlinghouse.

NATHAN ANDREW - b. 6 Jun 1932; s/o George Howard & Mildred (Jones) Garlinghouse. m. Brenda (...).

NELDA LURADA - b. 7 Aug 1897, Madison, Jefferson Co., IN; d/o Ulysses Arthur & Mary Erskine (Davis) Garlinghouse. m. Elmer Forest Fretz 24 Feb 1921. m2nd. Glen D. Wright.

NELLIE (Littlefield) - b. 1871, Iowa; d. 30 Apr 1899, Hahnemann Hosp., Chicago, IL; Buried at Hopkinton, Iowa. m. Lyman Edwin Garlinghouse 6 Mar 1896.

NELLIE AMELIA - b. 21 Aug 1881, Shawnee Co., Kan; d/o Lucian Bonaparte & Matilda Ruth (Hanawalt) Garlinghouse. m. Edward S. Cowdrick, one child Ruth Elizabeth.

NELLIE BOTHWELL - b. Jun 1858, Allen's Hill, Ontario Co., New York; d. 2 Feb 1942, Allen's Hill, Ontario Co., New York; d/o John Nelson & Lucy West (Bothwell) Garlinghouse. She had been a school teacher for many years in Livonia, NY and other area schools. She died in the family homestead where she was born.

NELLIE LEE (Tomkins) - b. 26 Jun 1867; d. 1940, Homer, Mich; m. Raymond Edgar Garlinghouse 25 Jun 1884, Jackson, Mich, one child Valerie.

NELSON ASA - b. 6 Jan 1910, Allen's Hill, Ontario Co., New York; d. 20 Jun 1983, Rhinebeck, New York. He served during WW II in the Pacific Theatre; s/o Stoughton Tracy & Mary Henrietta (Deal) Garlinghouse. m. Helen Matilda (Vossbrinck) 9 Oct 1948, one child Kent Nelson.

NELSON DARIUS - b. 18 Jun 1875, Worthington, Iowa; d. 7 Sep 1877, Worthington, Iowa; s/o Darius Hill & Minerva Jane "Jennie" (White) Garlinghouse.

NELSON S. - b. May 1838, Richmond, Ontario Co., New York; d. 26 Feb 1904, Ann Arbor, Mich; He served during the Civil War from 10 Oct 1861 to 13 Mar 1863 as Private in Company K &

Company G in the 13th Regiment of New York Volunteers. His commanding officer was Lieutenant Mark; s/o Samuel S. & Orpha (Harrington) Garlinghouse. m. Mary E. Willitts 17 Oct 1867, Ann Arbor, Mich, children Ida E. and Frank W.

NERINE (...) - m. Bill Garlinghouse. Living at Olathe, CO in 1996.

NETTIE - b. Sep 1867, Canandaigua, New York; d. 2 Oct 1867, Canandaigua, Ontario Co., New York; d/o Charles A. & Mary Elizabeth (Hewitt) Garlinghouse.

NINA GRACE - b. 12 Oct 1888, Worthington, Iowa; d. 4 Apr 1889, Worthington, Iowa; d/o Darius Hill & Minerva Jane "Jennie" (White) Garlinghouse.

NITA CORA - b. 1904, Lewiston, Idaho; d/o Arthur Richard & Anna B. (Jones) Garlinghouse. m. F. C. Funke, children Jacqueline Rose, Felix Christopher and Ann Marie.

NORA - b. 29 Sep 1903, Montezuma, Colo; d. 29 Sep 1903, Montezuma, Colo; d/o Elias B. & Virda Ellen (Lucas) Garlinghouse.

NORMA KAY - b. 7 Jun 1937; d. young; d/o George L. & Dorothy (Rogers) Garlinghouse.

NORMAN - m. Donna (...). Living at Olympia, WA in 1996.

NORMAN FAYETTE "FRANK" - b. 23 May 1847, Ohio; d. 4 Dec 1923, Bakersfield, Kern Co., CA; He was killed in a street car accident. s/o Silas & Margaret (Reid) Garlinghouse. m. Ada (...) 16 Aug 1870, children Morris and Cyril.

NORMAN S. - b. 29 Mar 1868, Oregon; d. 9 Jan 1939, at The Kings Daughters Home, Alameda, CA; Buried at Modesto, CA. s/o Stephen &

Prudence W. (Howard) Sanders Garlinghouse.

ODILLIE "DELLA" - b. Mar 1877, Hillsdale, Vermillion Co., IN; d/o Cyrenus A. & Sarah A. (Jackson) Garlinghouse. m. Lewis Sweet 24 Dec 1894, Fountain Co., IN, children Vera and Allen.

OLIVE - b. 1859, Effingham Co., IL; d/o David Woodruff & Catherine (Garlinghouse) Garlinghouse. m. George R. Prescott 7 Oct 1876, Wyanett, Isanti Co., Minn., children Guy and Bert. m2nd. John Liscumb, children Norman, Emma and Tressie.

OLIVE (...) - m. Josiah Garlinghouse.

OLIVE (Palmer) - b. 1863, Kan; m. Sherman Fayette Garlinghouse 1885, children Wilbur, Fayette and Daughter b. & d. 1897.

OLIVE D. - b. 26 Dec 1889, Arcade, New York; d/o Arthur L. & Sarah M. (Baker) Garlinghouse.

OPAL - b. 1872, Topeka, Shawnee Co., KS; d/o George C. & Hellin (Salisbury) Garlinghouse.

ORAL C. (Whitney) - b. 6 Mar 1887, Sunbury, Delaware Co., Ohio; d. Delaware Co., Ohio; m. Earl Leo Garlinghouse 11 Nov 1908, Delaware Co., Ohio, children Leland, Mervyn W. "Bud" and Mildred.

ORENZO CLAY see LORENZO

ORESTES LUCIAN,M.D. - b. 18 Jun 1870, Shawnee Co., Kan; s/o Lucian Bonaparte & Matilda Ruth (Hanawalt) Garlinghouse. m. Pearl Amy (Clark)

27 Sep 1899, children Marjorie Pearl, Lucian Clark and twins, Richard Earl and Robert Orestes.

ORIN - b. 1836, Licking Co., Ohio; s/o Gamaliel & Esther (Belknap) Garlinghouse. m. Sarah J. "Sally" (...).

ORPHA (Harrington) - d. 1843, Richmond, New York; m. Samuel S. Garlinghouse, children Darius Hill, Mary Ann, Nelson S., Franklin R., Peter and Phoebe.

ORPHA MARIE - b. 22 Aug 1877, Worthington, Iowa; d. 15 Dec 1930, Sand Springs, Iowa; d/o Darius Hill & Minerva Jane "Jennie" (White) Garlinghouse.

ORVA - b. about 1906, CA; d/o Orville & Violet (...) Garlinghouse.

ORVILLE - b. Mar 1873, CA; s/o Stephen & Prudence W. (Howard) Sanders Garlinghouse. m. Violet (...), children Orva, Myrna, Helen M., Stephen and Ileen.

OSCAR - s/o ... Garlinghouse. m. Daisy (...). Living at Fortuna, CA in 1996.

OSCAR ROSS - b. 30 Nov 1894, Marcus, IA; d. 15 Jan 1958, Detroit Lakes, MN; s/o Edmund Oscar & Sarah (Wilson) Garlinghouse. m. Margaret (Hammer) 30 Nov 1926, one child Edwin Oscar.

OTTO GATES - b. Oct 1885, Tecumseh, Lenawee Co., Mich; d. 1947; s/o Gurdon Benedict & Minnie Minerva (Gates) Garlinghouse. m. Tib (Hodges).

OWEN LEE - b. 5 Aug 1921; d. 12 Jan 1945; s/o Edward Sylvester & Emma (Shae) Garlinghouse.

OWEN WALTER - b. 1870, Emporia, Lyon Co., Kan; d. 16 Jan 1895, Kansas City, MO; Buried at Emporia, Kan. s/o Lewis N. & Nancy Jane

"Jennie" (Lockerman) Garlinghouse. m. Oct 1894, Emporia, Kan.

P. (...) - m. Ira G. Garlinghouse. Living at Delray Beach, FL in 1996.

P. (...) - m. ... Garlinghouse. Living at Livermore, CA in 1996.

P. (...) - m. Donald Garlinghouse. Living at Marysville, OH in 1996.

P. (...) - m. Albert A. Garlinghouse. Living at Dickinson, TX in 1996.

PAMELA JEAN (Hollingsworth) - b. 1945; m. Peter Lynn Garlinghouse 26 Apr 1973, children Brian and Betsy Lynn.

PARKER- b. May 1844, IN or Ohio; d. 15 Jan 1845, Delaware Co., Ohio; s/o Benjamin & Catherine Maria (Williams) Garlinghouse.

PATRICIA (Rowberry) - m. Jennings Bryan Garlinghouse 17 Oct 1946, one child Toni Ann.

PATRICIA (...) m. Bruce Garlinghouse. Living at Boulder, CO in 1996.

PATRICIA ANN (Spaulding) - m. Loren Ira Garlinghouse 1951, children Rick Loren and Cynthia Ann.

PATRICIA E. - d/o Harold James & Catherine M. (Spence) Garlinghouse, m. ... Smith.

PATRICIA ELOISE - b. 17 Mar 1926; d. Dec 1992, Panorama City, CA; d/o Edward Sylvester & Emma (Shae) Garlinghouse. m. Jerrold Davis, one child Gwen.

PAUL A. - Living at Austin, TX in 1996.

PAUL RAY - b. 13 Aug 1957, Cedar Rapids, IA; s/o Edwin Oscar & Betsy Jean (Anderson) Garlinghouse

PAULINA JANE - b. 20 Sep 1846, Switzerland Co., IN; d/o George Bennett & Isabella Jolly (DeWitt) Garlinghouse. m. Charles W. Humphrey 24 Dec 1863, IN, children Dau.(died as infant), George, Homer, Clara F., Clarence, Ardie M. and Jennie G.

PEARL - b. 1887; d. 1915; d/o Isaac Ashton & Hattie (Cory) Garlinghouse. m., one child Mildred Juanita.

PEARL AMY (Clark) - b. 21 Jul 1872, Kan; d. May 1968, Topeka, Kan; m. Orestes Lucian Garlinghouse, M.D. 27 Sep 1899, children Marjorie Pearl, Lucian Clark and twins Richard Earl and Robert Orestes.

PEGGY JEAN - b. 1949; d/o Junior Ellsworth & Lucy (Gascho) Garlinghouse.

PENNY SUE - b. 1961; d/o Lyle Rapheil & Elizabeth (Cemer) Garlinghouse.

PETER - b. 1805, Richmond Twp., Ontario Co., New York; d. young; s/o Benjamin & Anne (Morehouse) Garlinghouse.

PETER - b. Twin to Phoebe; d. in infancy; s/o Samuel S. & Orpha (Harrington) Garlinghouse.

PETER LYNN - b. 12 Feb 1948, Cedar Rapids, IA; s/o Edwin Oscar & Betsy Jean (Anderson) Garlinghouse. m. Pamela Jean (Hollingsworth) 26 Apr 1973, children Brian and Betsy Lynn.

PETER MARK - b. 25 Apr 1985, Topeka, Shawnee Co., Kan; s/o Whitney Beard & Nancy Ruth (Manus) Garlinghouse.

PHILIP - b. about 1970, Madison, Wisc; s/o Ralph Spalding & Ellen (Ekman) Garlinghouse.

PHOEBE - b. Twin to Peter; d. in infancy; d/o Samuel S. & Orpha (Harrington) Garlinghouse.

PHYLLIS MARGUERITE - b. 1927; d. 1968; d/o John Raymond & Genevieve May (Aldread) Garlinghouse. m. Gordon Barber.

POLLY "Mary" (Benjamin) - b. 8 Apr 1782, NJ; d. after 1865, Urbana, Steuben Co., New York; She was buried at Mt. Washington Cem., Steuben Co., NY. m. Thomas Garlinghouse 4 Oct 1801, Sussex Co., NJ, children Maria, David, Ethalinda, Joanna "Ann," Jane, Daniel Benjamin, Amy, Thomas and John Benedict.

POLLY - d/o Daniel Benjamin & Sarah "Sally" (Margeson) Garlinghouse.

PRUDENCE W. (Howard) - b. 10 Jan 1846, MO; d. 15 Apr 1934, Stanislaus Co., CA; m. ... Sanders. m2nd. Stephen Garlinghouse 1866, children Norman S., Isabel A., Orville, Lois E. and Cecil R.

R. (...) - m.... Garlinghouse. Living at San Diego, CA in 1996.

RACHEL - b. 16 Jan 1805, Ontario Co., New York; d. 18 Aug 1869, Philomath, Benton Co., Oregon; d/o James & Elanor "Eleanor" (Hunt) Garlinghouse. m. Abiather Vinton Newton 5 Oct 1826, Hardin Co., KY, children Kezia, Norris Peter, Isaac H., Cynthia Ellen, Corlista Tamar, Gamaliel Garlinghouse, Jasper and Mahala J.

RACHEL - b. 1838, Licking Co., Ohio; d/o Josiah & Amanda (Belknap) Garlinghouse.

RALPH B. - s/o ... Garlinghouse. m. Daisy (...). Living at New Baltimore, MI in 1996.

RALPH BASIL - b. 1930; s/o Elton Ellsworth & Leona (Beckman) Garlinghouse. m. Consuelo Hilda (Ramerz) 1952, children Elton Julian, Linda Mae, Brenda Jean and Deanna Lynn.

RALPH EDWIN - b. 6 Oct 1899; s/o Edmund Oscar & Sarah (Wilson) Garlinghouse.

RALPH LEMAN - b. 22 Jul 1889, Leadville, Colo; d. May 1982, Kaneohe, HI; s/o Holmes Spalding & Emma Permelia (Sherman) Garlinghouse. m. Elizabeth Hayes (Davison) 15 Nov 1919, Fresno, CA, children Nancy Elizabeth, Ralph Spalding and Grant Wesley.

RALPH SPALDING - b. 1926, Lihue, Hawaii; s/o Ralph Leman & Elizabeth Hayes (Davison) Garlinghouse. m. Ellen (Ekman) 1951, Batavia, IL, children Bruce, Ann, John Spalding and Philip.

RANDY JOHN - s/o Mark & Elizabeth Victoria (Pope) Garlinghouse.

RANDY L. - b. 1955; s/o Eugene Wayne & Bonnie (Crumback) Garlinghouse. m. Connie (Kreuger), one child Randy L., Jr.

RANDY L., Jr. - b. 1975; s/o Randy L. & Connie (Kreuger) Garlinghouse.

RAY ALDEN - b. 1931; s/o John Raymond & Genevieve May (Aldread) Garlinghouse. m. Donna Annalee (Hausler) 1953, children Darlene Louise, Darwin, Joyce and Michael.

RAYMOND- b. 16 Aug 1909; d. 9 Nov 1918; s/o Edward Sylvester & Emma (Shae) Garlinghouse.

RAYMOND EDGAR - b. 28 Mar 1860, Kan; d. 1940, Homer, Mich; Buried in Fairview Cem., Homer, Mich. s/o Abraham "Abram" & Agnes A. (Rose) Garlinghouse. m. Nellie Lee (Tomkins) 25 Jun 1884, Jackson, Mich, one child Valerie.

R. B. - Living at Midland, MI in 1996.

REBECCA (Stout) - b. 1 Mar 1827; d. 9 Oct 1867, Clifton Springs, New York; Buried in Old Cemetery, Mt. Morris, New York. m. ... Hawley. m.2nd ... Poyntell. m.3rd Joseph Garlinghouse, Jr.

REBECCA D. (...) - m. Larry Garlinghouse. Living at Odessa, TX in 1996.

REGENIA (DeBando) - m. Lorenzo Clay Garlinghouse 10 Feb 1887, Jefferson Co., IN.

REGGIE - s/o ... Garlinghouse. Living at Azusa, CA in 1996.

REID - b. 1867-68; s/o William & Elizabeth (Huff) Garlinghouse. m. Sue E. "Lou" (Miller) 22 Mar 1888, children Frank, Ruth, LaVey,

Eunice, Frederick Paul and Eva Jean.

RENA - b. 1907, Clarkston, Wash; d. B/4 1979; d/o Gerald Arza & Elizabeth (Gilbert) Garlinghouse. m. ... Zirbel about 1930, children William and Wendy G.

REUBEN S. - b. 20 Mar 1816, Richmond Twp., Ontario Co., New York; d. 28 Mar 1816, Richmond Twp., Ontario Co., New York; s/o Joseph & Submit (Sheldon) Garlinghouse.

R.G. (...) - m. Robert Garlinghouse. Living at Des Moines, IA in 1996.

RHODA - d/o Lacy & Elizabeth (McCormick) Garlinghouse. m. ... Taylor.

RHODA F. (...) - m. Fred "Fredie" Garlinghouse, Jr.

RHODA HARRIET (DuPey) - b. about 1857, Sault Ste. Marie, Mich; Buried at Alexandria, SD; m. Jasper Sylvester Garlinghouse 30 Oct 1876, Minn, children Cynthia A., Dolly, Edward Sylvester and a dau. who d. at 3 mo. m2nd. Erastus Taylor.

RHODELIA ANN - b. 4 Apr 1845, Delaware Co., Ohio; d. 28 Feb 1858, Van Buren Co., Iowa; Buried in White Chapel Cem., Van Buren Co., Iowa. d/o Silas & Margaret (Reid) Garlinghouse.

RICHARD - b. 31 Mar 1894; d. 13 Jul 1963, Brooklyn, New York; s/o Frederick L. & Ida (Tomkins) Garlinghouse. m. Ethyl (...) 1945. m2nd. Mabel (...) 1961.

RICHARD - s/o Monroe Garlinghouse.

RICHARD - s/o ... Garlinghouse. Living at San Francisco, CA in 1996.

RICHARD - s/o ... Garlinghouse. m. Eleanor

(...). Living at Colorado Springs, CO in 1996.

RICHARD - s/o ... Garlinghouse. m. Eldora (...) one child Dick. Living at Lewiston, ID in 1996.

RICHARD - s/o ... Garlinghouse. Living at Austel, TX in 1996.

RICHARD - s/o ... Garlinghouse. Living at Calistoga, CA in 1996.

RICHARD C. - s/o ... Garlinghouse. one child Rich C. Living at Sacramento, CA in 1996.

RICHARD EARL, M.D. - b. 5 Mar 1910, Kan; twin to Robert Orestes. s/o Orestes Lucian, M.D. & Pearl Amy (Clark) Garlinghouse. m. Miriam (Thoroman), children Richard Earl, Jr. and Gretchen Ann.

RICHARD EARL, Jr. - b. 12 Apr 1940; s/o Richard Earl, M.D. & Miriam Esther (Thoroman) Garlinghouse. m. Margaret Ann (Pettys) 23 Sep 1972, children Sarah McCall, Elizabeth Clark and Katherine Monroe.

RICHARD LYNN - b. 12 Apr 1907, Kan; d. 26 Apr 1988, Lewiston, Idaho; s/o Arthur Richard & Anna B. (Jones) Garlinghouse. Children Jac, Lynn and Sue Ellen.

RICH C. - s/o Richard C. Garlinghouse. Living at Sacramento, CA in 1996.

RICK - s/o ... Garlinghouse. m. Margaret (...). Living at Auburn, MI in 1996.

RICK LOREN - b. 1954; s/o Loren Ira & Patricia Ann (Spaulding) Garlinghouse. m. L. (...).

RILEY - b. 1839, Licking Co., Ohio; d. 1869, Topeka, Kan; s/o Gamaliel & Esther (Belknap) Garlinghouse.

RILEY - b. Ohio; s/o George & Sophronia (Sherman) Garlinghouse.

ROB - s/o ... Garlinghouse. Liiving at Edmond, OK in 1996.

ROBERT - s/o ... Garlinghouse. m. Louise (...). Living at Sterling Heights, MI in 1996.

ROBERT - s/o ... Garlinghouse. Living at Midland, MI in 1996.

ROBERT - s/o ... Garlinghouse. m. Melissa (...). Living at Lebanon, OR in 1996.

ROBERT - s/o ... Garlinghouse. Living at Ellenville, NY in 1996.

ROBERT - s/o ... Garlinghouse. Living at Hersey, MI in 1996.

ROBERT - s/o ... Garlinghouse. m. R. G. (...). Living at Des Moines, IA in 1996.

ROBERT BRUCE - b. 7 Oct 1958; s/o Bruce Beebe & Vivian Dickinson (Kabler) Garlinghouse. m. Diana (Morgan) 4 Feb 1984, children Katherine Marie Morgan and Allison Kabler.

ROBERT CRAIG - b. 22 Nov 1954, MI; d. Dec 1986, Detroit, Wayne Co., Mich; s/o Robert Vernon & Lorna May (Wagner) Garlinghouse.

ROBERT E. "Bob" - b. 22 Sep 1903, Lebanon, Montezuma Co., Colo; d. 19 Apr 1951; s/o Elias B. & Virda Ellen (Lucas) Garlinghouse. m. Ethel (Cash) 1926.

ROBERT ERWIN - b. 25 Oct 1917, Aitkin, Minn; d. 29 May 1985, Aitkin, Minn; s/o Edward Sylvester & Emma (Shae) Garlinghouse. He served in U.S. Army during W.W.2 (1941-1945). m. Agnes (Oakland) 6 Dec 1941, St. Paul, Ramsey Co., Minn, children Roberta Agnes, Nancy Jeanne, Thomas Lee and Colleen Joanne.

ROBERT LEE - b. 1922; s/o Fred Lee & Gertrude (Verheyen) Garlinghouse. m. Jean (...).

ROBERT ORESTES - b. 5 Mar 1910, Kan; d. Mar 1980, Rogers, Ark; he was twin to Richard Earl. s/o Orestes Lucian, M.D. & Pearl Amy (Clark), Garlinghouse. m. Esther Winifred (Coghill), children Mary Jean and Jane Esther.

ROBERT VERNON - b. 9 Apr 1930: s/o Vernon Lloyd & Margaret Lillian (Kaufman) Garlinghouse. m. Lorna May (Wagner) 6 Jan 1952, children Sandra Kay, Robert Craig, Kathy Ann, Gerald Lloyd and Julie Beth.

ROBERTA AGNES - b. 1942, Aitkin, Minn; d/o Robert Erwin & Agnes (Oakland) Garlinghouse. m. Howard Bodie, children Linda Marie, Kathleen Mary, Leah Jeanne and John Howard.

RODNEY - s/o Jennings Woodrow "Woodie" & Jeanne (...) Garlinghouse.

ROLAND - Living at Sanibel, FL in 1996.

ROLAND EDGAR - b. 11 Sep 1944, Pasadena, CA; s/o Leslie Holmes & Elizabeth Amy Westfall (Soults) Garlinghouse. m. Mary Gail (Bock) 30 Jul 1966.

RON - s/o ... Garlinghouse. Living at Pioneer, CA in 1996.

RONNIE - s/o Wallace Elias "Wally" & Betty (Finley) Garlinghouse.

ROSE EDITH (Justice) - b. 5 Apr 1892, Battleground, IN; m. Edward E. Garlinghouse 14 Oct 1909, Tippecanoe Co., IN, one child Edward H. C. m2nd. Oris Weston Black 16 Dec 1914.

ROSEMARY (Gutierrez) - b. 2 Jan 1952, Rockville

Centre, Nassau Co., New York; m. Kent Nelson Garlinghouse 12 Sep 1971, children Jason, Amanda Rose and Justin Asa.

ROY - b. 14 Jan 1919; d. Mar 1974, NJ; s/o Monroe Garlinghouse.

ROYAL EDSEL - b. 1929; s/o Elton Ellsworth & Leona (Beckman) Garlinghouse. m. Kathryn (Blanchard) 1950, children Sharon Kay, David Royal, Lynn Marie and Steven Roya5.

RUBY ELLA (Colwell) - b. 23 Jul 1921, Sault Ste. Marie, Chippewa Co., Mich; m. Lacy Grant Garlinghouse 31 May 1941, Sault Ste. Marie, Chippewa Co., Mich, children Dwayne Grant and Dean George.

RUBY MARY (Long) - b. 20 Jan 1939, Sault Ste. Marie, Mich; m. Jerry Louis Garlinghouse 20 Jun 1959, Sault Ste. Marie, Mich, children Donna Ruby, Connie Jean, Karen Lynn, Jeffrey Louis and Joseph Mark.

RUBY NELLIE - b. 20 Aug 1884; d/o Isaac Ashton & Hattie (Cory) Garlinghouse. m. Paul John Ginter, one child Don William.

RUTH - b. 8 Mar 1900, Ohio; d. Dec 1985, Beverly Hills, CA; d/o Reid & Sue E. "Lou" (Miller) Garlinghouse. m. W. L. Nutt.

RUTH - d/o Monroe Garlinghouse.

RUTH (Pettinger) - m. Frank Dewey Garlinghouse Jun 1925, one child Frank Dewey, Jr.

RUTH (Huckabay) - b. at Colony, Okla; m. James Buell "Bub" Garlinghouse 16 Mar 1935, Cortez, Montezuma Co., Colo, children Edward Buell, James and Carolyn.

RUTH ETHELENE - b. 11 May 1926, Lewis, Montezma Co., Colo; d/o Elias Buell & Virda Ellen (Lucas) Garlinghouse. m. Donald Holmes

16 Sep 1944, one child Larry. m2nd. Boyde Burton Bruning 6 Aug 1950, children Daralyn Ruth, Leila Dianne, Darwin Boyde and Lottie Marie.

SALLY - b. 1800-1810, Ontario Co., New York; d/o John & Jane (Leonard) Garlinghouse. m. George Fox.

SAMUEL - s/o Thomas & Lucy Emeline (Ludy) Garlinghouse.

SAMUEL DAYTON - b. 8 May 1880, Worthington, Iowa; d. 15 May 1953, Portland, Oregon; s/o Darius Hill & Minerva Jane "Jennie" (White) Garlinghouse. m. Belle (McBride) 1 May 1902, children Elmer George and Fern L. m2nd. Ada E. (Schmidt) Sep 1913, children Zona Pauline and Elaine Lurcil.

SAMUEL R. - b. 1831, New York; d. Jun 1879, Naples, Ontario Co., New York; s/o Stephen A. & Elizabeth "Betsy" (Roberts) Garlinghouse. m. Emily S. (Baker) Strowbridge Jan 1876, children Eugene and Grace June.

SAMUEL S. - b. 1797, New York; d. 1854; Buried in Purcell Road Cem., Richmond Twp., Ontario Co., New York. s/o Benjamin & Anne (Morehouse) Garlinghouse. m. Orpha (Harrington), children Darius Hill, Mary Ann, Nelson S., Franklin R., Peter and Phoebe.

SANDRA - d/o Morse Nolan & Dorothy Lillian (Roessell) Garlinghouse.

SANDRA KAY - b. 8 Jun 1953, MI; d/o Robert Vernon & Lorna May (Wagner) Garlinghouse. m. James Fry 27 Jun 1975.

SANDRA LEE - b. 11 Feb 1946; d/o Ace Nelson & Charlotte (Stone) Garlinghouse. m. Donald D.

Youngren, children Duane Donald and Kimberly Marie.

SANDY (...) - m. ... Garlinghouse. Living at Thompsonville, MI in 1996.

SARA (...) - m. David Garlinghouse, Jr. @ 1874, one child Evalyn "Eva".

SARAH "Sally" (Margeson) - b. 10 Jul1830; d. 21 Mar 1880; m. Daniel Benjamin Garlinghouse 22 Jul 1855, Steuben Co., New York, children Evaleen, Thomas Edison, Julia Ann, Grant, Alice Brundage and Polly.

SARAH McCALL- b. 26 Sep 1975; d/o Richard Earl, Jr. & Margaret (Pettys) Garlinghouse.

SARAH (Polhemus) - b. 4 Oct 1833, NJ; d. 22 May 1915, Newark, NJ; m. John Garlinghouse 24 Feb 1856, Newark, NJ, children George, Joseph, Ida and John.

SARAH (Wilson) - b. Kan; m. Edmund Oscar Garlinghouse 10 Jan 1894, children Oscar Ross, Hallie J., Ralph Edwin and Alvin Nathan.

SARAH (...) - m. ... Garlinghouse. Living at Sioux City, IA in 1996.

SARAH A. - b. 1840, Hart Co., KY; d/o George & Elcy Lee (Drury) Garlinghouse.

SARAH A. (Jackson) - b. 1842, Ohio; d. 22 Nov 1891, Vermillion Co., IN; m. Cyrenus A. Garlinghouse 1 Nov 1857, Ewington, IL, children Eliza Mae, Sylvester R., Alice "Allie", Franklin, Charles A. James, Jesse E. "Bessie", Lydia "Lidda" and Evaline M.

SARAH ANN "ESTHER" "SOPHINA" - b. 1817, New York; d/o James L. & Susannah (Belknap) Garlinghouse. m. Addison Carter 21 Dec 1837, Franklin Co., Ohio, one child Belanthus.

SARAH ANN (Ratcliff) - b. 1841, IN; d. Jul 1882, Peach Orchard, Clay Co., Ark; m. Andrew L. Garlinghouse 31 Jul 1856, Iowa, children Elias M., George M., Lenora Regina and a son. m2nd. John Oliver Weese 24 Nov 1866, Van Buren Co., Iowa, children John Henry, Howard R., Jesse, Rosa R., Sarah E. and Laura O.

SARAH ANN (Long) - b. Mar 1847, Kan or IN; d. 11 Nov 1922, Globe, Ariz; m. Martin V. Garlinghouse 28 Dec 1870, Augusta, Butler Co., Kan, children Minnie, Evalina Florence, Emma Kate, Cyrus Buell, Hattie and G. W.

SARAH C. - b. 9 Jul 1889, Newark, NJ; d. 6 Jun 1895, Newark, NJ; d/o Joseph & Cora Bell (Johnson) Garlinghouse.

SARAH ELAINE "Sadie" (Holmes) - b. Mar 1852, Orleans Co., New York; d. after 1922, Idaho; m. Arza H. Garlinghouse Mar 1873, children Arthur Richard, Gerald Arza, Hazel "Hec" "Hasel" Rupert and Georgia.

SARAH "Sally" E. (Cotton) - b. @ 1844, IN; d. 6 Apr 1906, Jefferson Co., IN; m. George Perry Garlinghouse, 16 Mar 1864, Switzerland Co., IN, children William DeWitt, Hattie "Netta" and Viola.

SARAH ELIZABETH - b. 24 Jul 1799, Ontario Co., New York; d. 18 Sep 1852, Naples, New York; d/o Benjamin & Anne (Morehouse) Garlinghouse. m. Joseph French 12 Dec 1824, children Julia, Joseph M., Peter, Phoebe, Mary, Freeman, Leonard Briggs, Isabel and Maria.

SARAH JEANNETTE - b. 18 Nov 1897, Madison, Jefferson Co., IN; d. 6 May 1985, Orlando, Orange Co., FL; d/o Lorenzo Clay & Serelda Catherine (Ashley) Garlinghouse. m. Daniel A. Farley 10 Oct 1916, Indianapolis, Marion Co., IN, one child Horace Whitcombe.

SARAH M. (Baker) - m. Arthur L. Garlinghouse, children Olive D., Leon "Leman" B., Layman, a dau. b. 2 Jan 1895 and Fred Lee.

SARAH MCCALL - b. 26 Sep 1975; d/o Richard Earl, Jr. & Margaret Ann (Pettys) Garlinghouse.

SCOEY - s/o ... Garlinghouse. Living at Port Townsend, WA in 1996.

SCOTT - s/o ... Garlinghouse. Living at Arroyo Grande, CA in 1996.

SERELDA CATHERINE (Ashley) - b. 2 Sep 1870, Owen Co., KY; d. 27 Oct 1948, Madison, Jefferson Co., IN; m. Lorenzo Clay Garlinghouse 12 Sep 1894, Jefferson Co., IN, chilren Serena Catherine and Sarah Jeannette.

SERENA CATHERINE - b. 7 Feb 1895, Madison, Jefferson Co., IN; d. 1950, Madison, WI; d/o Lorenzo Clay & Serelda Catherine (Ashley) Garlinghouse. m. Edwin Gordon Clarke 1913, Indianapolis, Marion Co., IN, children Lois Joan and Marjorie Caroline.

SERENA LUVADA - b. 4 Apr 1868, Madison, Jefferson Co., IN; d/o George Bennett & Serena Milton Boyd (Crusan) Garlinghouse. m. John C. Eckert 24 Nov 1886, children John Howard, Robert Rea, Henry Dale and Mary Serena.

SERENA MILTON BOYD (Crusan) - b. 21 Apr 1828, Brown Co., OH; d. 9 Sep 1912, Madison, IN; m. George Bennett Garlinghouse 6 Jan 1864, Ripley Co., IN, children Lorenzo Clay, Willard Elmer, Serena Luvada and Ulysses Arthur.

SHARON KAY - b. 1952; d/o Royal Edsel & Kathryn (Blanchard) Garlinghouse.

SHERIDAN - b. 1906, Kinross, Chippewa Co., MI; d. 1943; s/o Ulysses Grant Garlinghouse.

SHERIE - b. 1954; d/o Eugene Wayne & Bonnie (Crumback) Garlinghouse. m. Timothy DeCarve, one child Danielle.

SHERMAN - b. 1873, Mille Lacs, Minn; d. 1961, Maryland; s/o David Woodruff & Catherine (Garlinghouse) Garlinghouse. m. Ella (...), children Dorothy Margaret and Irene May.

SHERMAN - b. 21 or 29 Oct 1886, Leadville, Colo; d. 29 Oct 1886, Leadville, Colo; s/o Holmes Spalding & Emma Permelia (Sherman) Garlinghouse.

SHERMAN FAYETTE - b. 1851, Licking Co., Ohio; d. 1909; s/o George & Sophronia (Sherman) Garlinghouse. m. Mattie (Cheatham), children daughter, Valnor C. and Leon. m2nd. Olive (Palmer) 1885, children Wilbur and Fayette.

SHERMAN GRANT - b. 18 Sep 1921, Aitkin Co., Minn; s/o William Josiah & Elizabeth Howe (Campbell) Garlinghouse. m. Deloris Patricia (Shotts), children Lester David and William Harry.

SHERWOOD BENJAMIN - b. 25 Aug 1880, Vernon, Sussex Co., NJ; d. 1 Jan 1976, Vernon, Sussex Co., NJ; s/o John Monroe & Jesteen D. (Farber) Garlinghouse. m. Elizabeth (DeGraw) 9 Sep 1900, children David Bryan and John J. m2nd. Edith Geiss.

SHIRLEY ANN - b. about 1924; d/o Bryan Hess & Bertha T. (Gerrels) Garlinghouse. m. ... LeDuc. m2nd. Max Zaler.

SHIRLEY MAE - b. 10 Oct 1929; d. 13 Mar 1930; d/o Carroll & Velma Mae (Shirkey) Garlinghouse.

SILAS - b. 13 Jan 1809, Ontario Co., New York;

d. 8 Jul 1898, Winfield, Kan; s/o James & Elanor "Eleanor" (Hunt) Garlinghouse. m. Margaret (Reid) 1 Nov 1832, Delaware, Ohio, children William, Melissa Eliza, Calista Emily, Lewis N., Stephen, Arthelia Jane "Jennie", George, Rhodelia Ann, Norman Fayette, Alta Maria, Julia Ellen, Hiram and Martha Elizabeth. Shortly after the Civil War, the family moved by boat down the Ohio River, then by the Mississippi and Missouri Rivers, to Kansas. Their boat caught fire, and they lost most of their possessions on the Missouri River. They rented a farm for a year to raise crops, then continued to Kansas. At age 71, Silas and his wife Margaret moved to Oregon. Five years later they moved back to Kansas.

SILAS - b. 1832, Hart Co., KY; d. 11 Jul 1853, Hart Co., KY; s/o George & Elcy Lee (Drury) Garlinghouse.

SILAS - b. 18 Apr 1843, Vernon, Sussex Co., NJ; d. 7 Mar 1851, Vernon, Sussex Co., NJ; s/o John & Catherine Elizabeth (Utter) Garlinghouse.

SILVIE M. - b. 15 Mar 1892, Hillsdale, Vermillion Co., IN; d. 1976, Hillsdale, IN; d/o Sylvester R. & Lizzie White (Casebeer) Garlinghouse. m. Curtis Stewart 17 Mar 1912, children Annabelle and Philbert "Phillip".

SOPHRONIA (Sherman) - b. 1817, VT; m. George Garlinghouse 10 Sep 1840, Licking Co., Ohio, children Emery, Lucian Bonaparte, Cynthia, Sherman Fayette, Dawn Jane and Riley.

STACI DAWN - b. 1963, Lewiston, Idaho; d/o Jac Garlinghouse.

STEPHEN - b. @ 1769, NJ; s/o James & Joanna (Buchanan) Garlinghouse. He lived in Chemung per 1790 Federal Census of Montgomery Co., New York. He was listed as Stephen

Gardenhouse (sic). Probable children were Kiziah and Deborah.

STEPHEN - b. 9 May 1839, Ohio; d. 12 Jan 1914, Stanislaus Co., CA; s/o Silas & Margaret (Reid) Garlinghouse. m. Prudence W. (Howard) Sanders 1866, children Norman S., Isabel A., Orville, Lois E. and Cecil R.

STEPHEN - b. @ 1917, CA; s/o Orville & Violet (...) Garlinghouse.

STEPHEN A. - b. 1796, New York; s/o Benjamin & Anne (Morehouse) Garlinghouse. m. Elizabeth "Betsy" (Roberts) 1824, children Hosita "Harriett", Lincina "Lucina", Elsmond, Samuel R. and Truman.

STEVEN ROYAL - b. 1959; s/o Royal Edsel & Kathryn (Blanchard) Garlinghouse.

STOUGHTON TRACY - b. 18 Jun 1863, Allens, Hill, New York; d. 4 Jul 1947, Allens Hill, New York; s/o John Nelson & Lucy West (Bothwell) Garlinghouse. m. Mary Henrietta (Deal) 22 Oct 1902, Allens Hill, New York, children Leonard Deal and Nelson Asa.

SUBMIT (Sheldon) - b. 17 Apr 1791, Vermont; d. 12 Apr 1861, Auburn, New York; Buried in St. Paul's Churchyard, Allen's Hill, Ontario Co., New York. m. Joseph Garlinghouse 12 Oct 1808, Williamstown, Mass, children Jane, John Nelson, Leman Benton, Reuben S., William S., Laura, Joseph, Jr., Louise A., Mary, Ellen and Amelia S.

SUBMIT S. - b. about 1814, Ontario Co., New York; d/o John G. & Lewanna "Louanna" (Bennett) Garlinghouse. m. Willard S. Cobb 19 Sep 1830, Tippecanoe Co., IN, children Sophronia, Sarah G., Perlina E., Emma C., Marietta Eliza and Alice M. m2nd. Joseph Israel 25 Nov 1852, Switzerland Co., IN.

SUE (...) - m. ... Garlinghouse. Living at Fairmont, Minn in 1996.

SUE (...) - m. ... Garlinghouse. Living at Ft. Townsend, WA in 1996.

SUE E. "Lou" (Miller) - b. @ 1871; m. Reid Garlinghouse 22 Mar 1888, Delaware Co., Ohio, children Frank, Ruth, LaVey, Eunice, Frederick Paul and Eva Jean.

SUE ELLEN - b. 1950, Lewiston, Idaho; d/o Richard Lynn Garlinghouse. m. Eric ...

SUSAN (Moody) - m. John G. Garlinghouse about 1860, Switzerland Co., IN, one child Charles A.

SUSAN (Osborne) - b. 27 Apr 1845; d. 10 Nov 1871; m. Thomas D. Garlinghouse 9 May 1863, Florida, New York, children Charles and Flora.

SUSAN b. 5 Nov 1940, Detroit, Wayne Co., Mich; d/o John G. & Helen (Bulkley) Garlinghouse. m. Anthony J. Morse 1965, children Anthony J., Jr. and Caroline.

SUSAN - b. 13 Jul 1946; d/o Arnet John & Jean (Stewart) Garlinghouse. m. John Kuhn 1971.

SUSAN BUDER (Horan) - b. 28 Jun 1942; m. Bradley Kent Garlinghouse @1965, children Kimberly Anne, Marjorie Elise, Joseph Mark, Bradley Kent, Jr. and Matthew David.

SUSAN LEE - b. 7 Feb 1947, Pasadena, CA; d/o Leslie Holmes & Elizabeth Amy Westfall (Soults) Garlinghouse. m. Jerry Wayne Robinson 18 Sep 1970, one child Susan G.

SUSANNAH (Belknap) - b. 26 Jan 1792, Cherry Valley, Otsego Co., New York; d. 15 Feb 1841, Plains Twp., Franklin Co., Ohio; She was twin to Jesse Belknap. m. James L. Garlinghouse

"Jr.", children Arthur, Josiah, Benjamin, Jesse, Esther "Sarah Ann", Juliette and Ann Eliza "Elizabeth."

SUSANNAH "ROSANNA" - b. 9 Oct 1833, Licking Co., Ohio; d. Oct 1898, Thurston Co., Wash; Buried in Rochester Grand Mound Cem. d/o Josiah & Amanda (Belknap) Garlinghouse. m. Paul Groff 9 Mar 1852, Wapello Co., Iowa, children George, Gittio, Ida, Mary, Walter, Eldora, Mafor and Harriet.

SYLVESTER R. - b. 28 Nov 1858, Effingham, IL; d. 1 May 1930, Hillsdale, Vermillion Co., IN; Buried in Helt's Prairie Cem., Vermillion Co., IN. s/o Cyrenus A. & Sarah A. (Jackson) Garlinghouse. m. Ella (Orahood) 6 Aug 1879, Fountain Co., IN. m2nd. Lizzie White (Casebeer) 21 Feb 1883, Vermillion Co., IN, children LeRoy, Hugh A., Silvie M. and Georgia May.

TAMMI - b. 1960: d/o Donald L. & Joann B. (Nicol) Garlinghouse.

TERRI - b. 1958; s/o Donald L. & Joann B. (Nicol) Garlinghouse.

TERRY - s/o George William & Florence (Schultz) Garlinghouse.

THOMAS - b. 27 Aug 1773, Sussex Co., NJ; d. 10 Apr 1845, Urbana, Steuben Co., New York; buried Mt. Washington Cem., Steuben Co., NY. Prob. s/o James & Joanna (Buchanan) Garlinghouse. He was a wagon maker. m. Polly "Mary" (Benjamin) 4 Oct 1801, Sussex Co., NJ, children Maria, David, Ethalinda, Joanna "Ann", Jane, Daniel Benjamin, Amy, Thomas and John Benedict.

THOMAS - b. 1800, Vernon, Sussex Co., NJ; d. young; Buried in the United Methodist Churchyard, Vernon, Sussex Co., NJ. s/o Gamaliel & Mary (Monroe) Garlinghouse.

THOMAS - b. 8 Mar 1822, Sussex Co., NJ; d. 31 Jan 1896; s/o Thomas & Polly "Mary" (Benjamin) Garlinghouse. m. Lucy Emaline (Ludy) 25 Sep 1871, Washtenaw Co., Mich, one child Samuel.

THOMAS BRIGGS - b. about 1818, IN; s/o John G. & Lewanna "Louanna" (Bennett) Garlinghouse. m. Augusta (Demmett) 1847, children Louise and Harriet.

THOMAS D. - b. 2 Nov 1827, Vernon, Sussex Co., NJ; d. 19 May 1886, Warwick, NY; s/o Gamaliel

& Mary (Monroe) Garlinghouse. m. Susan (Osborne) 9 May 1863, Florida, New York, children Charles and Flora.

THOMAS EDISON - b. 11 Sep 1856, Wayne, Steuben Co., New York; d. 20 Dec 1859, Wayne, New York; s/o Daniel Benjamin & Sarah "Sally" (Margeson) Garlinghouse.

THOMAS GRANT - b. 12 Oct 1919; d. 18 Jan 1943; s/o Edward Sylvester & Emma (Shae) Garlinghouse.

THOMAS LEE - b. 1951, Aitkin Co., Minn; s/o Robert Erwin & Agnes (Oakland) Garlinghouse. one child Tom.

THOMAS SHERMAN - b. 1967, Pasadena, CA; s/o Albert Frederick & Barbara Evlyn (Myers) Garlinghouse.

TIB (Hodges) - m. Otto Gates Garlinghouse.

TILDEN WILLARD - b. 1 Jul 1880; s/o Willard Elmer & Fanny (Shears) Garlinghouse. m. Alma June (Weber).

TIM - s/o Timothy & Dawn (...) Garlinghouse. Living at Marysville, Ohio in 1996.

TIMOTHY DONALD - s/o Donald L. & Joann B. (Nicol) Garlinghouse. m. Dawn (...), one child Tim.

TINA (...) - m. ... Garlinghouse. Living at Aberdeen, WA in 1996.

TOM - s/o Thomas Lee Garlinghouse. Living at Long Lake, Minn in 1996.

TOM - Living at St. Paul, MN in 1996.

TONI ANN - d/o Jennings Bryan "Biggin" "Tex" & Patricia (Rowberry) Garlinghouse. m. Frank Nevis, children J. B. and Andrew.

TRACY LYNN d/o Lyle David & Barbara L. (Owens) Garlinghouse. m. ... m2nd. Adam Iaquinta children Christopher Garlinghouse, by 1st marriage and Ashley by 2nd marriage.

TREVA - d/o Jeremiah "Gerald" & Bessie (...) Garlinghouse. m. Earl Pearson/Pierson.

TREVA - b. 26 Jul 1917, Hillsdale, Vermillion Co., IN; d/o Hugh A. & Eva O. (Watson) Garlinghouse.

TRUMAN - b. 1840, New York; s/o Stephen A. & Elizabeth "Betsy" (Roberts) Garlinghouse.

ULYSSES ARTHUR - b. 2 Nov 1871, Madison, Jefferson Co., IN; d. 9 Oct 1949, Ft. Wayne, Allen Co., IN; s/o George Bennett & Serena Milton Boyd (Crusan) Garlinghouse. m. Mary Erskine (Davis) 20 Sep 1894, Madison, Jefferson Co., IN, children Nelda Lurada, Arlene Ruth and Henry Elmer.

ULYSSES GRANT - b. 2 Apr 1864, Effingham Co., IL; d. 27 Oct 1933, Sault Ste. Marie, Mich; s/o David Woodruff & Catherine (Garlinghouse) Garlinghouse. m. Gertrude (Harrison), Aitkin, Minn. m2nd. Dora (Harrison), Aitkin, Minn. m3rd. Mable (...), Aitkin, Minn. m4th. Adeline (King) 24 Mar 1891, Kinross, Mich. Ulysses sired Charlotte, Leslie, Joseph, Alice, Edith, Amanda, Mark, Sheridan, Lacy Grant, Earl and Martha.

VALERIE - b. 25 Apr 1885, Homer, Mich; d. 1970; d/o Raymond Edgar & Nellie Lee (Tomkins) Garlinghouse. m. John Milo Barr, children two daughters who died in infancy and Bonita June.

VALERIE (Johnson) - b. 12 Sep 1895; d. 7 Apr 1973, Big Springs, Howard Co., TX; m. George Lovette Garlinghouse.

VALNOR C. - s/o Sherman Fayette & Mattie (Cheatham) Garlinghouse. m. Irene (Reynolds).

VELDA (...) - m. Gerald Garlinghouse. Living at Spokane, WA in 1996.

VELMA MAE (Shirkey) - b. 18 Sep 1903; m. Carroll Garlinghouse, children Shirley Mae, Carroll Ellsworth, Earl Alonzo and Ardyce Loraine.

VERNON - b. 20 Apr 1894, Vernon, Sussex Co., NJ; d. 1947, Vernon, NJ; s/o John Monroe & Jesteen D. (Farber) Garlinghouse. m. Mabel (Flood), children Margaret and Vernon.

VERNON - s/o Vernon & Mabel (Flood) Garlinghouse. m. Marie (Parker), children Cindy and Debbie.

VERNON LLOYD - b. 5 Aug 1906, Spokane, WA; s/o John Edward & Effie Gertrude (Perrine) Garlinghouse. m. Margaret Lillian (Kaufman) 1928, children Robert Vernon, Eugene Wayne and Margaret Lee.

VICKY (...) - b. 29 Nov 1921; d. Oct 1980. Des Moines, Iowa; m. ... Garlinghouse.

VIOLA - b. 1869, Iowa; d/o Lacy & Elizabeth (McCormack) Garlinghouse.

VIOLA - b. 1877, IN; d/o George Perry & Sarah "Sally" E. (Cotton) Garlinghouse.

VIOLA - d/o Bryan Hess & Bertha T. (Gerrels) Garlinghouse. m. ... Edmonds, children Althea, and Louise Marie.

VIOLA L. - b. 13 Mar 1901, Homer, Calhoun Co., Mich; d/o Charly "Charles" Abram & Louise (Hess) Garlinghouse.

VIOLA MARIAH - b. 12 Aug 1857, IN; d/o George Bennett & Isabella Jolly (DeWitt) Garlinghouse. m. George F. Stiver 16 Oct 1879, Jefferson Co., IN, children George A. and John.

VIOLET (...) - b. 1878, CA; m. Orville Garlinghouse, children Orva, Myrna, Ellen M., Stephen, and Ileen.

VIRDA ELLEN (Lucas) - b. 17 Oct 1883, Joplin, MO; d. 17 Sep 1969, Colo; m. Elias Buell Garlinghouse 11 Nov 1901, Cortez, Colo., children Robert E., Nora, Dora E., Leonard, James Buell, Mary May, Benjamin Porter, Jennings Woodrow, Jennings Bryan, George William, Wallace Elias, Virda Marie, Martin, LeRoy and Ruth Ethelene.

VIRDA MARIE - b. 17 Aug 1920, Lewis, Montezuma Co., Colo; d. 5 Jun 1945, Cortez, Montezuma Co., Colo; d/o Elias Buell & Virda Ellen (Lucas) Garlinghouse. m. Marvin L. Harmon 7 Jan 1935, children Shirley Marie, Gerald, Dean, Linda Arleen, and Sandra Sue.

VIVIAN - d/o George B. & Josie (Robison) Garlinghouse.

VIVIAN DICKINSON (Kabler) - b. 29 Jul 1931, San Diego, CA; m. Bruce Beebe Garlinghouse 22 Mar 1952, San Francisco, CA, children William John, Robert Bruce, Julie Ann and Carrie Lee.

WALLACE - s/o George B. & Josie (Robison) Garlinghouse.

WALLACE ELIAS - b. 9 Jan 1919, Lewis, Montezuma Co., Colo; d. 6 Oct 1989, Santa Maria, CA; s/o Elias Buell & Virda Ellen (Lucas) Garlinghouse. m. Betty (Finley), one child Ronnie.

WALTER SHELDON - b. Mar 1854, Canandaigua, Ontario Co., New York; He served as Sergeant in the 8th Cavalry & the 3rd Cavalry stationed at Fort Clark near Bracketville, Kinney County, TX from 20 Feb 1879 to 19 Feb 1889 during the Indian Wars on the Texas-Mexican border; s/o Leman Benton & Martha Ann (Spalding) Garlinghouse. m. Julia Annie (Alder) 12 Mar 1884, Eagle Pass, TX, children Walter Sheldon, Jr., Clara "Carrie", Arthur Alder and Lily.

WALTER SHELDON, Jr. - b. 10 May 1885, Ft. Clark, Kinney Co., TX; d. 3 Jul 1973, Titusville, Brevard Co., FL. He is buried in Ridgewood Cemetery, Glenview, Cook Co., IL; s/o Walter Sheldon & Julia Annie (Alder) Fisk Garlinghouse. m. Eugenia "Jennie" (Meisel) 18 Jan 1911, Chicago, Cook Co., IL, children Ferdinand Walter and Charles Albert.

WALTER SHELDON, III - b. 9 Jun 1960, Orlando, Orange Co., FL; s/o Arthur Alder & Dora (Reyna) Campillo de Garlinghouse. m. Donna Marie (Schwieter), Knoxville, Tenn children Kevin Michael and John Edward.

WANDA LEILANA - b. 1960, Boulder, Colo; d/o

Grant Wesley & Barbara Irene (Frame) Garlinghouse.

WEBB MARK - b. 3 Jun 1944; s/o Francis Mark & Marjorie Cosper (Beard) Garlinghouse. m. Julie Ann (Haidish), one child Katherine Elizabeth.

WENDELL LEWIS - b. 14 Jun 1908, Topeka, Kan; d. 3 Jun 1993, Topeka, Kan; Buried in Mt. Hope Cem., Topeka, Kan. He served in US Army during WW II. s/o Lewis Fayette & Katherine (Fogwell) Garlinghouse. m. Ella Helen (Skadeen) 16 Mar 1940, children Anne Patricia and David Clarke. m2nd. Imogene (Boggs).

WHITNEY BEARD - b. 16 Jun 1949, New York, NY; s/o Francis Mark & Marjorie Cosper (Beard) Garlinghouse. m. Nancy Ruth (Manus), children James Manus, Whitney Christopher and Peter Mark.

WHITNEY CHRISTOPHER - b. 6 Oct 1982, Topeka, Shawnee Co., Kan; s/o Whitney Beard & Nancy Ruth (Manus) Garlinghouse.

WILBUR - b. 1893, Kan; s/o Sherman Fayette & Olive (Palmer) Garlinghouse.

WILHELMINE "WILMA" EMILIE (Menzen) - b. 27 Dec 1916, Gary, IN; m. Charles A. Garlinghouse 16 Oct 1944, Detroit, Wayne Co., Mich, children Gail Wilma and Janet Elizabeth.

WILLARD - b. Nov 1883, Maybrook, New York; d. 20 Aug 1959; buried in Warwick Cem., Warwick, Orange Co., NY. s/o James & Anna (Bennet) Garlinghouse. m. Martha Josephine (Morris) about 1908. Children John, Rolf, and Effie.

WILLARD ELMER - b. 13 Oct 1865, Allensville, Switzerland Co., IN; d. 16 Dec 1928, Madison, Jefferson Co., IN; s/o George Bennett & Serena Milton Boyd (Crusan) Garlinghouse. m. Fanny (Shears) about 1880, one child Tilden

Willard. m2nd. Mary Elizabeth (Ashley) 8 Apr 1891, Jefferson Co., IN, children Florence Luanna, Ella Murat, Ida Elena and George Howard.

WILLIAM - b. 5 Aug 1833, Ohio; d. 1909, Johnstown, Licking Co., Ohio; Buried at Johnstown, Licking Co., Ohio. s/o Silas & Margaret (Reid) Garlinghouse. m. Elizabeth (Huff) 1 Dec 1853, Delaware, Ohio, children Emerson, Mary F., George E., William E. and Reid. m2nd. Mrs. Mary Ann (Coyle) Jones 23 Sep 1885, Lane Co., Oregon.

WILLIAM "Bill" - s/o George William & Florence (Schultz) Garlinghouse.

WILLIAM "Bill" - s/o ... Garlinghouse. m. Cathy (...). Living at Sonoma, CA in 1996.

WILLIAM - b. 1968, Ellenville, NY; s/o Edward Joseph & Jane (Russell) Garlinghouse.

WILLIAM - s/o ... Garlinghouse. Living at Michigan City, IN in 1996.

WILLIAM - s/o ... Garlinghouse. Living at Olathe, CO in 1996.

WILLIAM DEWITT - b. 1865, IN; d. Jefferson Co., IN; s/o George Perry & Sarah "Sally" E. (Cotton) Garlinghouse.

WILLIAM E. - b. about 1863, Ohio; s/o William & Elizabeth (Huff) Garlinghouse. m. Luella (Crego) 2 Dec 1885, Delaware Co., Ohio, children Earl Leo, Leland Eugene and Howard.

WILLIAM EDWARD - b. 1851-52, Canandaigua, New York; s/o Leman Benton & Martha Ann (Spalding) Garlinghouse.

WILLIAM H. - b. Nov 1873, Wapello Co., Iowa; s/o James H. Garlinghouse.

WILLIAM HARRY - b. 22 Sep 1943, Centralia, Wash; s/o Sherman Grant & Deloris Patricia (Shotts) Garlinghouse.

WILLIAM JOHN - b. 17 Mar 1955, Wilmington, Del; He is an Ensign in the US Navy. s/o Bruce Beebe & Vivian Dickinson (Kabler) Garlinghouse. m. Judy (Glascock) 19 Nov 1983, children Christopher Thomas and Joseph William.

WILLIAM JOSIAH - b. 1 Mar 1867, Princeton, Aitkin Co., Minn; d. 3 Aug 1936, Gates, Thurston Co., Wash; s/o David Woodruff & Catherine (Garlinghouse) Garlinghouse. m. Elizabeth Howe (Campbell) 1900, children James Rufus, Frank, Frances, Earven, Bessie, Ella Mae, Bud and Sherman Grant.

WILLIAM L. - b. 1916-17, in Wheatfield, near Globe, Ariz; s/o Cyrus Buell & Minnie (Lee) Garlinghouse. m., one child Leon.

WILLIAM - Living at Show Low, AZ in 1996.

WILLIAM S. - b. 1 Jun 1817, Richmond Twp., Ontario Co., New York; d. 25 Jun 1817, Richmond, New York; s/o Joseph & Submit (Sheldon) Garlinghouse.

ZOE E. - b. 1890, Delaware Co., Ohio; d/o Reid & Sue E. "Lou" (Miller) Garlinghouse.

ZONA PAULINE - b. 12 May 1914; d/o Samuel Dayton & Ada E. (Schmidt) Garlinghouse. m. Jay Gordon Gookstetter 14 May 1942, children Jeri Lynn, Wendy Ann and Kristi Ada.

INDEX OF ALLIED FAMILIES

ABEARE
Iva Mable 14,66,81,
92,94
ADAMS
Almeda May 47
Dennis 47
Florence A. 47
Florence Luanna 47
Harry R. 47
James Deray 47
Jerry 111
Jesse Denmore 47
John Wickersham 47
Joseph Lanier 47
Nancy Jeanne 111
Patrick Michael 111
Ray 47
Thomas Mitchell 111
ALDER
Julia Annie 8,23,81,
145
ALDREAD
Genevieve May 17, 52
77,120,127
ALLEN
Emma L. 42
Richard M. 42
Tracy 42
ANDERSON
Betsy Jean 14,26,35
119
George 95
Lucretia D. 95
ANDREWS
Carrie Lee 18
Thomas C. 18
ARBUCKLE
Floyd 107
Mary May 107
ARMSTRONG
Alice 3
Elsie Lee 40, 90, 95
Ferne Beatrice 3,46,
99 100
Floyd 3
ASHLEY
Mary Elizabeth
39,47,53,63,105,147
Serelda Catherine
93,131,132
AVERY
Cynthia A. 24
F. Christopher 24
BACON
Esther A. 42
BAKER
Emily S.
41,44,56,129
Sarah M.
9,49,87,88,115,132
BALL
Carol Jean 17
Kathleen 17
Kelly Kristin 17
Walter 17
BARBER
Gordon 120
Phyllis Marguerite
120
BARR
Bonita June 142
John Milo 142
Valerie 142
BARRETT
Lucy 95
BASKWELL
Minnie 21,109

BEAL
Amy Clark 70
Jane Esther 70
BEARD
Marjorie Cosper
14,48,101,146
BEARDSLEY
Chloe Rebecca
7,22,77,79
BECKMAN
Leona 11,40
88,96,121, 127
BEEBE
Leona Mae 8,15,89
BEKES
Barbara Leigh 11
Gerald Allen 11
Joseph Anthony 11
Michael Joseph 11
Stephanie Ann 11
BELKNAP
Amanda 4,19, 60,
69,80,103,121,137
Amazilla 19
Catherine 19
Corrington Gavitt 69
Eleanor 104
Electa 104
Elijah 19
Esther 19,24,42,51
52,116,125
Gamaliel 19
George 69
Hannah 69
Harley Augustus 69
James Mitchell 19
Jane 19,55
Jesse 5,69
Jonas 19
BELKNAP, con't.
Jonas Newton, Jr 104
Joseph Gillett 19
Kesiah 69
Lafayette 19
Mary Ann 104
Mary Jane 19,86,106
Orin 104
Rachell 104
Ransom Amos 55,69
Samuel 19
Susannah 6,8,12,68
72,80,82,130,136
Talitha Cumi 69
BENEDICT
Mary Jane 13,16,57,
75,136
BENJAMIN
Polly 5,26,27,43,69
73,75,100,120,138
BENNER
Eliza May 37
Zachery T. 37
BENNET
Anna 6,44,64,104,146
BENNETT
Lewanna 6,12,25,28,
53,65,76,91,135,138
BERG
Carl 73
Jesse Mabel 73
BERGSTROM
Beverly 35
Cecil 35
Deanna 35
Eileen Edna 35
BLACK
Margaret L. 99
Oris Weston 126
Rose Edith 126

BLANCHARD
Diane 92
Dick 92
Donna 92
Kathryn 28,83,97
127,133,135
Linda 92
BLOOM
Margaret 98
BOCK
Mary Gail 105,126
BODIE
Howard 126
John Howard 126
Kathleen Mary 126
Leah Jeanne 126
Linda Marie 126
Roberta Agnes 126
BOGGS
Imogene 64,146
BOMAR
Crispin S. 58
Hannah 58
Thomas E. 58
BONE
Betty Lois 14,88
BOREN
Clara Mae 55
Georgia May 55
Roy O. 55
Wilma 55
BOTHWELL
Lucy West 1,2,42,46
77,80,95,112,135
BRADBURN
America J.
5,36,53,61
BRADEY
Amanda 4
H. Wesley 4,5
BREWER
Homer C. 99
Margaret C. 99
BRIGGS
Adelaide 2
Barzillai T. 103
Donald G. 2
Elnathan 2
Leonard B. 103
Mary 103
Rodney N. 2
Thomas 103
Whitney 2
BRINKMAN
Edward 44
Eva 44
Lillian 44
BROOKS
Villa A. 1
BROWN
Lanah 86,93
BRUCE
Elizabeth Jane Allen
15,34,38
BRUNNING
Boyde Burton 128
Darwin Boyd 128
Deralyn Ruth 128
Leila Diane 128
Lottie Marie 128
Ruth Etheline 128
BRYAN
Mrs. Francis M.
48,57

BUCHANAN
Joanna 1,12,51,67,
73,74,78,98,134,138
BULKLEY
Helen 76,136
BUSHONG
Almina Tillie 4
L. Bittle, MD 4
Mina Ruth 4
BUTLER
Annette Lee 100
Daniel Leonard 100
Dawn Marie 100
John Vernon 100
Leonard 100
Leonard Warren 100
Margaret Lee 100
CALL
David G. 94
Lovina 94
Martha B. 94
Mary Jane 94
Mathew R. 94
Nancy M. 94
CAMPBELL
Bill 33
Edith 33
Elizabeth Howe 13,15
33,38,39,47,48,69,
133,148
Hazel 33
CAMPILLO
Dora 31,145
CANODE
Carol 17
CARD
Emma 41,63,68,74
Ethel 28,61,143
CAROTHERS
Frank P. 95
Lucretia D. 94,95
CARR
Lily 92
William B. 92
CARTER
Addison 6,130
Belanthus 130
Carol 17
Robert 17
Sarah Ann 130
CASEBEER
Lizzie White 55,62,
89,92,134,137
CASH
Ethel 43,125
CASTILLIO
Dora Reyna 8
CEMER
Elizabeth 29,38,87,
96,119
CHAFFIN
Carol 8,17
CHAPLINE
Elinor J. 36
J.B. 36
CHASE
Cynthia A. 24
Elsie Sophia 40
CHEATHAM
Mattie 88,108,133,
142
CHRISTIAN
Dorothy Jean 32,33
CLARK
Pearl Amy 94,101,
115,119,124,126

CLARKE
Edwin Gordon 132
Lois Joan 132
Marjorie Caroline 132
Serena Catherine 132
COBB
Alice M. 135
Emma C. 135
Marietta Eliza 135
Perlina E. 135
Sarah G. 135
Sophronia 135
Submit S. 135
Willard S. 135
COCKBURN
Cora M. 24, 48
COCKERELL
Emanuel 108
Lewis 108
Melissa Eliza 108
Nathan 108
COGHILL
Esther Winifred 43,70,107,126
COGSWELL
Carrie Lulu 90
Henry F. 90
Jennie Violettie 90
Lettie 90
COLLARD
Anna M. 103
Caroline Ophelia 103
Mary 103
Samuel 103
Sarah 103
Susan Feagles 103
Thomas T. 103
COLLINS
Mary 104
COLWELL
Ruby Ella 29,32,86 127
COMSTOCK
Addie 63
Alice M. 69
Delphine 69
Emma 63
Henry 63
Henry, Jr. 63
Ida 63
Isabel 69
Jane 69
Louise B. 103
Mary 103
Orville 103
Pinckney 69
Samuel 69
Verndella 63
CORY
Hattie 59,65,88,119, 127
CORYELL
Margaret Jane 26,27, 65,75,90,99
Melissa A. 7,43,65, 75,108
COTTON
Sarah E. 54,59,131, 143,147
COURTER
Ellen 20,39
COWDRICK
Edward S. 112
Nellie Amelia 112
Ruth Elizabeth 112

COYLE
Mary Ann 104,107
William 104
CRAMER
George P. 108
Melissa A. 108
CREGO
Luella 33,62,87,
96,147
CRUMBACK
Bonnie 14,22,44,
86,122,133
CRUSAN
Serena Milton Boyd
53,93,132,141,146
DAVIS
Ella 39,48
Gwen 118
Gerrold 118
Mary A. 55,68,95,104
Mary Erskine 8,61,
106,112,141
Patricia Eloise 118
DAVISON
Elizabeth Hayes 38,
57,111,121
DEAL
Mary Henrietta 89,
106,112,135
DeARMOND
Ella Murat 39
Fred 39
DeBANDO
Regenia 93,102
DeBRULER
Mary 49,95
DeCARVE
Danielle 133
Sherie 133
Timothy 133
DECKER
Garrett 85
Kiziah 85
DeGRAW
Elizabeth 28,37,76,
133
DelPOZO
Estela 42,90
DEMETT
Augusta 9,59,93,138
DERTZ
Ellen D. 60
John G. 60
DEVERS
Margueritte Menair
100
DeVERTER
Frances 47,61
DeWITT
Isabella Jolly
10,21,47,53,54,66,
76,91,119,143
DEXTER
Daniel 95
Lucy Lee 95
Walter Franklin,Jr
95
Walter Franklin, Sr.
95
DILLON
Katherine 21
DIVILBISS
Minnie L. 54,109
DOCHTERMAN
Kristin Elizabeth
111
Lloyd Bryan, Major
111
Nancy Elizabeth
111

DODGE
Elizabeth 37
Otis 37
DONAHO
Janet Elizabeth 70
Richard 70
DOUGLAS
Jessie E. 73
DOWNEY
Ellen Courter 20,39
DOYLE
Ruby 48
DRURY
Elcy Lee 36,47,51, 52,58,65,68,75,90, 102,108,130,134
DuPEY
Ella Jane 27,39
Rhoda Harriet 24,30 35,71,123
ECKERT
Henry Dale 132
John C. 132
John Howard 132
Mary Serena 132
Robert Rea 132
Serena Luvada 132
EDMONDS
Althea 143
Louise Marie 143
Viola 143
EDWARDS
Janet Elizabeth 70
Mark 70
EIGHNEY
Margaret L. 99
William 99
EKMAN
Ellen 6,15,39,77, 120,121
EVERETT
Carol Jean 17
Ronald 17
FALK
Donna 30,84,108
FARBER
Jesteen D. 48,71, 73,74,77,83,110,133, 142
FARLEY
Daniel A. 131,132
Horace Whitcomb 132
Sarah Jeannette 131
FARRISH
Marjie 101
FERGUSON
Mrs. Imogene Shaw 12,64
FICEK
Darlene Louise 27
Shyla Marie 27
Steven Thomas 27
William 27
FINCH
Joanna 73
John 73
Julia 73
Ornan B. 73
FINLEY
Betty 13,126,145
FISK
Albert 81
Julia Annie 8,23,81
Lorenzo J. 81
FITZPATRICK
Amelia Florence 5, 25,40,88
FLOOD
Mabel 98,99,142

FOGWELL
Katherine 48,83, 91,146
FOREWOOD
Elizabeth E. 38
Manual 38
Viola 38
FORGERSON
Frank A. 83
Katherine Elizabeth 83
FORTENBACH
Cortland P. 63
H. 63
Ida 63
L.B. 63
FOX
George 129
Sally 129
FRAME
Barbara Irene 11,57 84,146
FRANK
Dorothy Margaret 32
Lawrence 32
FREDERICKS
Lorraine 3,17,50,93
FRENCH
Barzillai 81
Benjamin 81
Freeman 131
Harriet 81
Horace 81
Isabel 131
James 81
Joseph 131
Joseph M. 131
Julia 131
FRENCH, con't.
Julia Ann 81
Leonard Briggs 131
Maria 131
Mary 131
Peter 131
Phoebe 131
Sara 81
Sarah Elizabeth 131
FRETZ
Elmer Forest 112
Nelda Lurada 112
FRY
James 129
Sandra K. 129
FUNKE
Ann Marie 113
F. C. 113
Felix Christopher 113
Jacqueline Rose 113
Nita Cora 113
FURMAN
Judy 65
GARD
Amy Lou 101
Marjorie P. 101
Spencer A. 101
GARDENHOUSE
Henry 60
GARNS
Mable 98
Walter 98
GASCHO
Lucy 5,52,75,82, 95,119
GATES
Minnie Minerva 8,23,43,57,109,116

GEISS
Edith 33,133
GELVIN
Florence Evelyn 73
Grover G. 73
Jesse Mabel 73
John W. 73
Mabel Elizabeth 73
Melvin L. 73
Myrtle E 73
William 73
GERRELS
Bertha T. 13,15,133 143
GILBERT
Cynthia A. 24
Elizabeth 19,30,37, 55,101,110,123
Franklin 24
Orin 24
Sireno 24
GILMAN
Arabella Louise 7
Lemuel O., Lt. Col. 7
GILPATRICK
Mary Ellen 50,105, 111
GINTER
Don William 127
Paul John 127
Ruby Nellie 127
GLASSCOCK
Judy 22,80,81 148
GOETZ
Hilda 28,61
GOOKSTETTER
Jay Gordon 149
Jeri Lynn 149
Kristi Ada 149
Wendy Ann 149
Zona Pauline 149
GRADY
Lilly M. 2,6,49,60, 91
GRAHAM
Clayton 43
Etha 43
GRAY
Margaret C. 13,16, 76,99
GREENSTEIN
Curtis 65
Hyman 65
Irene 65
GRINDLE
Cynthia 24
David 24,45
Evelyn 45
Vern 43
GROFF
Eldora 137
George 137
Gittio 137
Harriet 137
Ida 137
Mafor 137
Mary 137
Paul 137
Susannah 137
Walter 137
GUEMSTE
Diane Russell 30
Russell 30

GUTHRIE
Edward 99
Margaret 99
GUTIERREZ
Rosemary 5,70,
82,127
HAIDISH
Julie Ann 83,146
HAMILTON
Helen D. 60
Mart 60
HAMMER
Margaret 35,99,
116
HANAWALT
Matilda Ruth 4,35,
54,64,91,94,107,
112,115
HARMON
Gerald Dean 143
Linda Arleen 143
Marvin L. 143
Mary Elizabeth 82
Sandra Sue 143
Shirley Marie 143
Virda Marie 143
HARRINGTON
Orpha 27,49,104,
113,116,119,120,
129
HARRISON
Dora 31,141
Gertrude 21,55,141
HARTMAN
Lynn 46,96
HARTZELL
Ada 2
H.M. 2
HAULENBECK
Eliza 36
Emma 36
Henry 36
Isaac P. 36
HAUSLER
Donna Annalee
27,31,80,108,122
HAWLEY
Rebecca 79,122
HADEN
Laura Elma 4,58,87
HEBERGER
Elsie Sophia 40,89
HEBERHARDT
Bess 13
Hugh 13
HELM
David 83
Kathleen 83
HERMON
Mary Elizabeth 105
HESS
Louise 15,22,93,143
HEWITT
Mary Elizabeth
20,105,113
HIGH
Marybelle Price
90,107
HILL
Edna M. 34
HILLIARD
Mary Inez 77,78,106
HILTON
Agnes 95
Allen 95
Drothy 95

HILTON, con't.
Gladys 95
Homer Allen 95
John Herbert 95
Lott 95
Lucretia D. 94,95
Mary 95
HOAGLAND
Fanny B. 46
Frank 46
HODGE
Clifford 39
Ella Mae 39
HODGES
Tib 116
HOLLINGSWORTH
Pamela Jean 14,15, 118,119
HOLMES
Donald 128
Larry 128
Ruth Etheline 128
Sarah Elaine 9,54, 55,59,131
HOPKINS
Elizabeth 37
Orville H. 37
Socretes Nelson 37
Victor Nelson 37
HORAN
Susan Buder 14,15, 80,85,101,108,136
HORNER
Ann Elizabeth 6
Elias 6
HOUGHTON
Alfred Augustus 17
Caroline 17
Edith 17
HOUGHTON
Katherine Martha 17
Marion 17
HOUT
George L. Alexander 94
Harmon 94
Lovina 94
Sherman M. 94
Wesley 94
William S.
HOWARD
Prudence W. 20,66, 92,114,115,120
HUCKABAY
Ruth 18,34,68,69,127
HUDDLESTON
Dennis Gregg 57
Gretchen Ann 57
Zachery Clark 57
HUFF
Elizabeth 37,41,53, 105,122,123,147
HUMPHREY
Ardie M. 119
Charles W. 119
Clara F. 119
Clarence 119
George 119
Homer 119
Jennie G. 119
Paulina Jane 119
HUNT
Elanor 19,35,36, 51,52,58,67,69, 101,104,121,134
IAQUINTA
Adam 140
Ashley 140
Tracy Lynn 140

IKENBERRY
Evalina Florence 45
Flora 45
INSKEEP
Albert 24
Clyde 24
Cynthia Emily 24
Emma Lulu 24
Grace 24
Isaac Newton 24
Maude 24
Ralph 24
ISRAEL
Hellen 60,76
Joseph 135
Submit S. 135
JACKSON
Sarah A. 3,21,24, 37,45,49,68,73,96, 115,130,137
JACOBUS
Amzi N. 103
Anna 103
Augustus 103
Clarence 103
Cornelius H. 103
Emma 103
Herman 103
Mary 103
Mary Estelle 103
Ransford 103
Sarah 103
Spencer 103
Wallace 103
JARVIS
Lucretia D. 95
JOHNSON
Abigail 1
Andrew 1
Betsy 1
Cora Bell 23,56,63, 79,131
Georgia Ann 51,55
Jane 1
Johanna 1
John 1
Marjorie 90, 101
Valerie 54,142
JONES
Anna B. 6,9,52, 113,124
Arthur 63
Elizabeth Victoria 38
Ida E. 63
Mary Ann 104,147
Mildred 13,53,54, 75,92,93,109,111
JONSSON
Esther 9,42
JUSTICE
Rose Edith 34,126
KABLER
Vivian Dickinson 15, 18,82,125,144
KAUFMAN
Margaret Lillian 44, 100,126,142,148
KENDRICK
Hazel O. 56,60
KIBBY,
Georgia May 55

KING
Adeline 2,141
Harold 60
Helen 60
KINGSBURY
Carrie May 18,54
KIRKENDALL
Calista Emily 17
Cora 17
George 17
Matthew W. 17
Omer A. 17
KIRKHAM
Joseph M. 91
Lewanna 91
KNORR
Caroline S. 17,44, 47,53,56
KREUGER
Connie 23,122
KROLL
Betty Jo 13
Beverly Ann 13
Gloris Jean 13
Stanley 13
Stanley Andrew 13
Vicky Lee 13
KUHN
John 136
Susan 136
LACEY
Alfred 46
Flora 46
LAIRD
Irene 54,65
LANDERS
Ellen 39,91
LASCALZO
Esther 42
LAWRENCE
Arvilla 9
Janet 70
Kerry 70
LeDUC
Shirley Ann 133
LEE
Ada 31
Delbert 31
Dora E. 31
Edith 31
Elsie 31
H. L. 58
Hannah 58
L.J. 58
Minnie 25,109,148
Samuel Lindsey 58
Silas 58
Silas J.J. 58
Stanley 31
Wesley 31
LEONARD
Jane 12,37,68,69, 73,74,76,79,89,103, 129
LESLIE
Jeanette M. 71
LINNEMEIER
Arlene Ruth 8
Frederick Henry 8
LISCUMB
Emma 115
John 115
Norman 115
Olive 115
Tressie 115

LITTLEFIELD
Arthur Evan 72
Isaac Evan 72
Jennie May 72
Jennie Olive 72
Nellie 96,112
LOCKERMAN
Nancy Jane 13,31, 91,111,116,117
LONG
Doris Margaret 11, 29,31,50,83,96,101
Ruby Mary 2,3,31, 71,72,80,83,127
Sarah Ann 25,42, 45,51,59,102,109, 131
LOUDEN
Anah 7
Anna E. 7
Forest 7
Frances Cordelia 7
Frank J. 7
George 7
Ila 7
LOWE
Hugh John, Jr. 111
Margaret 111
Mary 111
Nancy Elizabeth 111
LOWRY
Archie 60
Hazel O. 60
LUCAS
Virda Ellen 12,31, 36,54,67,68,72,89, 102,107,113,125, 128,143,145
LUDY
Lucy Emaline 95,129 138
LUNCE
Ann Louise 34
David 34
Donald 34
Edith Esma 34
Elmer 34
Margaret 34
Mary 34
Robert 34
Ruth Ellen 34
LUPTON
Anita Rose 63
Don Allen 63
Earl 63
Earl Kieth 63
Ida Elena 63
Janice Lefern 63
MAHONEY
Eva 44,51,93
MANUS
Nancy Ruth 68,111 119,146
MARGUSON
Mary 26,48,65,103, 105
Sarah 3,26,45,56,81, 120,130,139
MARSH
Frank 58
George Wallace 58
Hannah 58
John 58
John Radley 58
Josephine 58
Mary Emma 58

MARTENS
Lola 35,92
MARTIN
Evaline J. 45
George 45
MASON
Marjorie 90,101
MAURER
Alta Maria 4
John D. 4
Maude 4
Ralph J. 4
Roland Blaine 4
Willis R. 4
McBRIDE
Belle 11,40,46,129
McCARTY
Hannah 58,68
McCLORY
Genevieve 52,87,
100
McCLURE
Mary E. 13,49,76,98,
105
McCORMICH
Alexander 65
Elizabeth 37,42,
50,61,63,65,80,
86,123,143
Irena Jane 65
James A. 65
Loanna 65
Thomas 65
William 65
McCULLOUGH
Mildred 109
McFADDEN
Josephine O. 21,76,
80
McFARLAND
Cynthia Ann 24
Jason Michael 24
Jerome Joseph 24
McGIBBEN
Karen 107
Kay 107
Kendra 107
Kenneth H. 107
Mattilda Cecile 107
McLAUGHLIN
Don 96
Lydia 96
Will E. 96
McNAIR
Marguerite 3,100
MEISEL
Eugenia "Jennie" 21,
44,46,145
MENZEN
Wilhelmine Emilie
("Wilma") 21,51,70,
146
MILLER
Bonnie Lou 94
Harold Ira 94
Harold Lloyd 94
Lovilla Gertrude 94
Ronald Lee 94
Sue E. 45,48,50,61,
87,127,136,149
MILLERN
Bessie 13
David 13
MILLS
Frederick P. 70
Frederick Peter Jr.
70
Jane Delphine 70

MITCHELL
Grace 28,56,94,106, 107
MOINI
Hilda 28,61
MONROE
Hattie 59
Mary 28,51,52,58, 67,74,102,103,138, 138
Willis 59
MONTGOMERY
Muriel Beatrice 8, 110
MOODY
Susan 20,136
MOORE
John Lemuel 88
John Lemuel, Sr. 88
Lenora Regina 88
MOREHOUSE
Anne 7,12,81,119, 129,131,135
MORGAN
Diana 4,29,83,125
MORRIS
Martha J. 102,146
MORSE
Anthony J. 136
Anthony J., Jr. 136
Caroline 136
Janet Marilyn 70,78
Susan 136
MYERS
Barbara Evlyn 3,11, 50,68,139
NEISWENDER
Mary 104
NEVIS
Andrew 139
Frank 139
J.B. 139
Toni Ann 139
NEWBERRY
Emma Kate 42
Leroy 42
NEWMAN
Laura 44,49
NEWTON
Abiather Vinton 121
Carlista Tamar 121
Cynthia Ellen 121
Gamaliel Garlinghouse 121
Isaac H. 121
Jasper 121
Keziah 121
Mahala J. 121
Norris 121
Peter 121
Rachel 121
NICHOLS
Alfred 93
Cassiah 19,24,25,45, 76,91,100,102
Louisa 93
NICOL
Jo Ann 30,73,138, 139
NOLAN
Hattie B. 59,68,77
NULF
Frances 47
Pearl H. 47
NUTT
Ruth 127
W. L. 127

OAKLAND
Agnes 2,23,111,
125,126,139
OBST
Ardyce Loraine 7
David Wayne 8
Herman G. 8
OLSON
Jeannette Madge 71
Oliver 71
ORAHOOD
Alice 3
Ella 38,137
Grace 3
Lillian G. 3
William H. 3
OSBORN
Susan 20,46,136
OURSLER
Cora 23,54,107,139
OWENS
Barbara L. 96,140
PALMER
Daniel 101
David 101
Filina 101
Martha 101
Olive 46,115,133,
146
Rufus 101
PARKER
Abigail 1
Anna 1
Marie 22,29,142
Nathaniel 1
PATTERSON
Charles A. 45
Evaline M. 45
PEARSON
Earl 140
Treva 140
PEASE
Audry 9
David 9
PERON
Dorothy 31
Jeane 32
PERRINE
Effie Gertrude 35,
40,64,75,77,142
PETTINGER
Ruth 48,127
PETTYS
Margaret Ann 38,83,
99,124,130,132
PHILIPS
Carrie A. 9,18,50
POLHEMUS
Sarah 52,63,74,79,
130
PONTON
Mary Ada 33,89,104
POPE
Elizabeth Victoria
14,29,30,38,50,72,88
101,122
POYNTELL
Rebecca 79,122
POWELL
Thomas 105
Mary Elizabeth 105
PRESCOTT
Burt 115
George R. 115
Guy 115
Olive 115

PRICE
Bertha E. 13,69
Marybelle 98,107
PROCHNOW
Clara 22,23
Fred 23
Julius R. 23
PROVOST
Charles 111
Nancy Jeanne 111
PYME
Jeanette 33,71
RAINEY
Ellen Jane 40
Janelle Jane 40
Jess Edwin 40
Robert J. 40
RAMERZ
Consuelo Hilda 15, 23,29,40,92,121
RASE
Amy Lu 81
Joyce Iva 81
Lisa Jo 81
Oscar Raymond 81
Raymond Vern 81
RATCLIFF
Frederick 72
Frederick Darius 72
Ida May 72
Jennie May 72
Jessie Mary Ann 72
John Edwin 72
Manley Lawton 72
Minerva Susanna 72
Nelson Frank 72
Orpha Grace 72
Sarah Ann 6,36,54,88 131
READ
Ann Eliza 43
Bertha May 13
Ellen J. 43
Ethalinda J. 48
Harold T. 13
Henry Thomas 13
Ira 43
Mary A. 43
Phoebe Maria 43
Rozilla 43
REAMON
Anne Patricia 7
Derek 7
Todd 7
REDMAN
Anthony 107
Cornelius 107
Evaline 107
Henry Sinclair 107
Levina 107
Mary Jane 106,107
Travis 107
REED
Esther Anna 21,42, 43,59,64,65
Fanny B. 46
George Pitts 46
REID
Lynn 97
Margaret 4,8,17,52, 61,82,91,98,102,108, 113,123,134,135,147
Seanna 97
REYNA
Dora 8,31,145
REYNOLDS
Irene 65,142

RICHIARDI
Gertrude 16, 55
RIDL
Jack R. 82
Julie Ann 82
ROBBINS
Abraham 36
Eleanor 36
Harmen 36
Lafayette 36
Rachel 36
Silas 36
Thomas 36
ROBERTS
Elizabeth 37,40, 61,92,129,135, 140
ROBERTSON
Anna M. 7,74
ROBINSON
Jerry Wayne 136
Susan G. 136
Susan Lee 136
ROBISON
Josie 40,53,60,80 143,145
ROESSELL
Dorothy Lillian 32, 78,110,129
ROGERS
Dorothy 31,54,77, 113
RORCK
Kay 69,84,98,110
ROSE
Agnes A. 1,2,22,89, 122
ROW
Ruby Ellen 33
ROWBERRY
Patricia 118,139
RUSSELL
Jane 30,34,35,70,147
RYERSON
Maria 19,36,39,74,79 93,100,103
RYSSO
Ernest Norbert 51
Gail Wilma 51
Jennifer Leigh 51
SABINS
Carol 17
Ronald 17
SAGER
Ida Mae 64
SALISBURY
Hellin 23,45,49,53, 60,115
SANDERS
Prudence W. 66,92, 114,115,120,135
SANGES
Hattie B. 59
W.A. 59
SATTERTHWAITE
Alice Brundage 3
C.A. 3
SAULIERE
Christy Lynn 22
Gregory 22
SARGENT
Lynn Evelyn 29,96, 97

SAYLER
Arthulia Jane 8
George B. 8
SCHAFF
Alva 107
Leroy 107
Mary May 107
SCHEDDEL
Beverly Ann 14
Gary Lee 14
Gregg Larry 14
Jack Lester 14
Jery Loren 14
Joel Larry 14
Larry Earl 14
Lori Ann 14
SCHMIDT
Ada E. 2,129,
149
SCHULTZ
Florence 47,54,
78,92,138,147
SCHWIETER
Donna Marie 3,75
84,145
SEMAN
Alice 4,75
SEATON
Mary Elizabeth 69,
105
SELCH
Charles E. 73
Herschell 73
Jessie E. 73
SHAE
Emma L. 3,34,35,
41,71,99,116,118,
122,125,139
SHAW
Imogene 12,64
SHEARS
Fanny 46,139,146
SHELDON
Corrine 16,24
Ellen 39
Harriet J. 94
Horatio G., Maj. 39
Louise A. 94
Submit 15,39,69,77,
79,87,88,94,103,123,
135,148
Walter G. 94
William Herold, Maj.
94
SHERMAN
Emma Permelia 3,42,
61,90,121,133
Sophronia 24,28,41,
52,94,125,133,134
SHIRKEY
Velma Mae 8,18,19,
33,133,142
SHOEMAKER
Grace 56
SHORT
Dale 64
Inez Florence 64
Janice Gail 64
Lorinda 7,70,77,93
Ronald Dale 64
SHOTTS
Deloris Patricia 29,
90,133,148
SHULL
George M. 70
Jane Delphine 70

SIMMONSEN
Keziah 29,85
SIMPSON
Emily 41
Esther Ellen 41
George Irvin 41
Georgia 41
Isaiah 41
Omer 41
Richard 42,54
Sarah Ann 41,54
SINDAL
Christopher 102
Mary 102
SKADEEN
Ella Ellen 7,28, 39,146
SMITH
Charles Huston 81
Foreste 47,49
Jennie 81
Julia Annie 81
Patricia E. 118
SOULTS
Elizabeth Amy Westfall 38,90, 126,136
SPALDING
Martha Ann 5,9, 17,20,50,61,88,101, 145,147
SPANGENBERG
Katherine Elizabeth 83
SPAULDING
Ida May 56,64,90,96, 99
Patricia Ann 24,92, 93,118,124
SPENCE
Catherine M. 19,35, 59,118
SPERRY
David Ralph 100
Donald Monfort 100
Katherine Ferne 100
Margaret Lee 99,100
SPILLMAN
Nancy Joyce 111
Rhinda Sue 111
William E., Jr. 111
STANLEY
Anna Louise 7
Edward Byron 7
STAPLES
Alice V. 103
Clarence 103
Cyrus 103
Eugene 103
Harriet 103
Herbert 103
John 103
John R. 103
Mary 103
Norris 103
Richard 103
STARK
Anne 7,102
STEBBINS
Julia Allerton 61, 77,81
STEED
Ann Elizabeth 6
Della 6
James 6
Melissa E. 6

STEPHENS
Carolyn 18
Ronnie 18
STEPHENSON
Margaret 53,64,
98,
STEWART
Annabelle 134
Curtis 134
Jean 8,70,71,83,
136
Julia C. 1
Philbert 134
Silvie M. 134
STIVER
George A. 143
George F. 143
John 143
Viola Mariah 143
STONE
Charlotte 1,17,21,
22,129
STOUT
Rebecca 79,122
STREMLAW
Katherine Elizabeth
83
William 83
STROWBRIDGE
Emily S. 41,129
Frank L. 41
Fred 41
Lyman 41
STUART
Eva 34,44,65,91
Julia C. 81
SWAIN
Christopher 100
Mariah 100
SWEENEY
Ethel M. 44
John D. 44
SWEET
Allen 115
Lewis 115
Odillie 115
Vera 115
TAYLOR
Gladys Grace 40,55,
87,90
John E. 95
Lucy Livings 95
Rhoda 123
Townsend John 95
TERHUNE
Catherine 19
John W. 19
Josephine 19
Ransfred 19
THOROMAN
Meriam 57,110,124
TIBERIUS
Anna Elizabeth 70
Charles Edward 70
Dennis E., Jr. 70
Janet Elizabeth 70
Leah Emilie 70
TIGNER
Dora Maude 31
Richard Alexander 31
TOMKINS
Ida 63,123
Nellie Lee 112,122,
142
TURNER
Lois Jane 92

ULRY
Juliette 82
Samuel 82
UTTER
Catherine Elizabeth 18,19,20,23,74, 76,77,134
VANCLEAVE
Laura M. 40,54,75, 87
VERHEYEN
Gertrude 49,55,126
VINING
Alice C. 75
VOSSBRINCK
Ellen Matilda 60,84
WAGNER
Lorna May 55,82, 84,93,125,129
WARD
Abigail Mary 1
Charles 1
Irene 1
WATERMAN
Jessie E. 89
Leona M. 89
William 89
WATSON
Eva O. 45,61,62, 98,110,140
WEBB
Amelia 5,6,52, 101,104
WEBER
Alma June 4,139
Charles Willard 47
Florence Luanna 47
James Lanier 47
Joseph Harding 47
WEBSTER
Albert 56
Byron Almond 70
Dorothy 56
Grace June 56
Gurdon Lathrop 70
Harold 56
Henry Louis 56
Jane 69
John Gurdon 70
Lester Garlinghouse 70
WEESE
Howard R. 131
Jesse 131
John Henry 131
Laura O. 131
Oliver 131
Rosa R. 131
Sarah Ann 131
Sarah E. 131
WELLER
Amelia Orvilla 5
Flora 5
Frances 5
Nathaniel 5
WHITE
Harriet 49,55
Minerva Jane 4,27, 34,42,71,96,109,112, 113,116,129
WHITNEY
Oral C. 33,87,108, 109,115
WIDER
Arthur 71
John 71
Myrtle 71
Raymond 71

WIDNER
Jennie C. 71
WILCOX
Ellen Linia 105
Ethaline Nora 104
Isaac Wilbur 104
Jennie Elvira 105
Jesse Fremont 105
Mary Ann 104,105
Orpha Adell 105
Ulrie Delgreen 105
WILLIAMS
Alice 3
Caroline Mary 18
Catherine Maria 1,9, 12,20,53,72,118
Ethel 18
Hazel 60
James H. 18
John Henry 18
John M. 18
Kittie Elizabeth 18
Libourne W. 3
Maude 8,108
Robert Albert 18
William E. 18
WILLITS
Mary E. 48,63,105, 113
WILSON
Clarissa Maye 23
Douglas Garlinghouse 23
Halleck Edward 23
Mary Jane 27,106
Sarah 4,34,58,116, 121,130
Virginia Edith 23
WITWER
Elizabeth Anne 107
John Price 107
Mary Jean 107
Robert Earl 107
WOLCOTT
Carrie 18,26,34,96
WOOD
Ellen 39
Georgeann 39
Stephen 39
William 39
WORLOCK
Beverly 14,59
WRIGHT
Glen D. 112
Nelda Lurada 112
YAGER
Carol 17
Jeffery A. 17
Jerry 17
Kelly Lynn 17
Scott T. 17
YINGLING
Axie Mable 10,18, 35,109
YOUNGREN
Donald D. 129,130
Duane Donald 130
Kimberly Marie 130
Sandra Lee 129
ZALER
Max 133
Shirley Ann 133
ZIRBEL
Rena 123
Wendy G. 123
William 123
ZOLMAN
C.E. 109
Mildred 109

www.ingramcontent.com/pod-product-compliance
Lightning Source LLC
Chambersburg PA
CBHW071125280326
41935CB00010B/1121

* 9 7 8 0 7 8 8 4 1 1 2 2 9 *